Praise for BOOBS, BOYS, AND HIGH HI

"Now that I've read Dianne Brill's book I'll neve dressed again. What a woman!"

—DEBORAH HARRY

"Want to know how you can turn heads, spin hearts, have the most fun ever, and sashay in the highest heels? Read *Boobs, Boys and High Heels* and you'll know it *all.*"

—GRACE JONES

"Dianne Brill and this book are like a walking, talking *Cosmo* cover—it's great to see someone having so much fun and celebrating her 'Babedom.' Go for it!"

—CINDY CRAWFORD

"Dianne Brill's book is brilliant! Especially the dating, romancing, and seducing tips."

—SINEAD O'CONNOR

"In this book Miss *Brill*iancy shows us how to let that Blond Factor . . . in everyone of us shine."

—TAYLOR DAYNE

"I have always admired Dianne Brill and now I know why!"

—TAMA JANOWITZ

"Ladies, grab your copy: no woman should be without this book. The fabulous Dianne Brill has unselfishly donated 208 pages of her ego-boosting babedom guidelines. This is now my reference book for feeling beautiful, inside and out. It's a celebration of womanhood and the power of femininity."

—JUSTINE BATEMAN

"Mademoiselle Bon-Bon, Miss Brill, has the most beautiful curves in the world! And, of course, I love her book! *Et voilà*!"

—JEAN-PAUL GAULTIER

"Dianne Brill is the shape of the nineties. She has reinvented the criteria of what is beauty today. In life, as in her book, she always keeps me smiling."

—THIERRY MUGLER

BOOBS, BOYS, AND HIGH HEELS

DIANNE BRILL, the siren of style. A designer/actress/model/business-woman and now author. She lives in Manhattan, works in Paris, L.A., Munich, London and has successfully developed her own time zone.

Dianne Brill

BOOBS, HIGH

OR HOW TO GET DRESSED

BOYS, & HEELS

IN JUST UNDER SIX HOURS

VERMILION
LONDON

First published in the UK in 1992 by Vermilion
an imprint of Ebury Press
Random House UK Ltd
20 Vauxhall Bridge Road
London SW1V 2SA

Second impression 1992

Catalogue record for this book is available from the British Library.

ISBN 0 09 177387 3

Cover artwork: Martin Lovelock

Printed and bound in Great Britain by
Butler & Tanner Ltd, Frome and London

THIS BOOK IS

DEDICATED TO MY MOM,

Noni Kendall Brill

THE MOST COMPLETE WOMAN

I'VE EVER KNOWN.

Grandiose thanks

TO EVERYONE WHO

MADE THIS BOOK HAPPEN—

AND *YOU* KNOW WHO YOU ARE!

ESPECIALLY TO MY BROTHERS

TROY, MICHAEL, AND JON,

AND SISTER MORRI.

ALSO ESPECIALLY TO RUDOLF.

AND, OF COURSE, TO MARCO PIRRONI,

JANIS SAVITT AND GARY BOGARD.

PLUS, TO MY COACH, AND MUSE,

NINA "SAY IT IN ENGLISH!" MALKIN.

ABOVE ALL, TO MY

STRONG AND COURAGEOUS "MR. LION."

Contents

BOOBS, BOYS, & HIGH HEELS

INTRODUCTION

Dianne Brill: A Body of Work

"I know you're really famous and everything . . . but what is it, exactly, that you *do*??????"

I've been hearing that question, politely phrased, for years. Sure, plenty of people have heard of my exploits as Queen of New York nightlife. You've seen photos of me on fashion runways and in splashy magazine spreads. Maybe you caught me on your favorite talk show or saw me in a movie. Perhaps you admired a great guy dressed in a suit that I designed. Or passed a boutique window and saw a life-size mannequin of me smiling out at you.

And still, you're wondering, she does so much . . . but what does she *really* do?

Of course, you know Dianne Brill. Big boobs. Big hair. Big smile. The curvy, buxom blonde in those ultraglam gowns and high heels. The babe who's everywhere: Paris, New York, London, L.A., Berlin, Tokyo, Milan.

Yet . . . who am I and what do I do?

I do it all.

I am a designer/actress/model/author/businesswoman. And through my multiple lives so far, I've had the opportunity to be a Queen in the international party tornado of fun and spend time with some of the world's most amazing men and women; with years of good tips to my credit (just ask my friends) it's made me a leading authority on romance and the art of being a contemporary Sex Goddess.

I was born in Racine, Wisconsin, raised in Tampa, Florida, and in a very short time became a name in New York City. Through strokes of self-marketing magic, the help of wonderful friends, major media support, and lots and lots of luck, I rose to prominence in a number of fields.

When I got started in business, I didn't understand the concept of "you can't do that," "you don't have the qualifications or experience," "that's impossible—it's never been done." Oh, really?

If you don't know "their" rules, you have no limitations. That has always been and continues to be my guideline for success. In work and in love. With friends and with lovers. From nightlife into daylife.

My first job was working in Tampa's most swingin' designer jeans store (back when designer jeans were the quintessential fashion imperative). Our mission, as the number-one-hottest, most important avant-and-groovy fashion sales force, basically, was to help squeeze patrons into skin-tight, gold-embroidered, rhinestone-studded jeans, then have them lie on the floor while we hooked key rings into the zippers and showed them how to zip them up. I was the top in sales, of course, and my best customers were members of the Tampa Bay Bucs football team.

Around that time, I decided to go to London for a week. I wound up staying for a year. I got a job as a makeup artist for a top cosmetics company (although I'd never been formally trained), traveling around Britain doing presentations and makeovers. I worked makeup magic on stage while the English lovelies watched, sipped tea, and politely applauded my chosen "befores" and "afters."

Before long, I lost interest in that career and took up something completely new: a sales job in the fashion faction of a brokerage house. Visa dramas with immigration when coming back to London after a business trip to Paris led me to leave Europe. You know, work permits pending, etc. I was almost deported. But I was told I could come back to the U.K. in six months.

Six months!?!?!?!?!?!

Nightmarish shock hit me. Tampa?! So soon? I knew I couldn't go back to the beach. I panicked. Then I calmed down. I got an idea. Antique clothing was trendy in London, so I figured it could be just as big in the U.S. I bought out a warehouse stocked with new-old (never worn) clothes and shoes (circa 1960s), packed them in some trunks, and brought them to New York City. I got out the phone book and looked under boutiques for some atmospheric names. Trash and Vaudeville. Manic Panic. The Zoo. Screaming Mimis. Patricia Field (the legend, I'd read about her in *Interview* mag). Then I started making business calls. Cold! Just walked into these trendy shops with samples of my stock stuffed into duffel bags. And they bought. Everything.

Okay. My stock was great. My prices were low. And the goods were immediately available. But there was another factor that helped my stuff sell. Me. I believed in what I was selling. Absolutely and wholeheartedly. I knew that this was the best gear going. And my conviction came through. Others believed it too. Did it matter that I didn't go to school to learn this or work my way through the ranks of the garment industry? No! To my delight, I realized that the key to making it in business was *believing* in what I had to offer. And I know this applies to just about every career and especially to love. Because without that unshakable belief, it doesn't matter if you're giving the stuff away . . . nobody will want it.

Eventually, my name got around. Soon I was exporting antique clothes to Japan, Sweden, everywhere. I was making good cash. The kind that spends. And fast! Another brainstorm: Put a fancy label in any garment and it gains credibility. So I formed a company and called it Classix (don't laugh, it was trendy at the time) Nouveau.

I was a businesswoman. A small but good one. And then I got creative. I started reconstructing the vintage garments. I'd take apart an entire "fat man's" suit and remake it, turning the jacket double-breasted and Spencer-length, adding leather trim, overdying the fabric, pleating the trousers, and fastening leather D-ring buckles to peg the pantlegs . . . completely redesigning the suit. That's how I developed my "destroy-to-create" design theory. Of course I had no traditional design training. If you want to know the truth, I got a D in home economics in junior high school.

I specialized in men's clothes. They were most easily available to me, and the most interesting to reconstruct. And, after all, being Dianne Brill, I wanted all the world's great guys to be my personal Ken dolls. I named my second company Gumex (after a Brazilian hair oil for men). Stores were buying my designs and selling them to very important customers. Prince, for instance, wore one of my reconstructed leather-trimmed trench coats in the movie *Purple Rain*. I did a small fashion show at my then-new-boyfriend Rudolf's club Danceteria. Next, I was flown to Japan with my menswear collection to present a huge fashion show sponsored by a major department store chain.

Slowly, I began working with pattern makers and tailors, designing my own menswear from scratch. I found an investor and formed company number three, Dianne Brill Menswear, Inc. The name of my first fully financed collection was The New Millionaires Club.

I launched The New Millionaires Club at a fashion show for six thousand (buyers and friends) at the Palladium in New York City. Forty-five gorgeous Brill Boys modeled my collection that night, among them artist Keith Haring and actors Billy Baldwin and Ian Buchanan. Another male model was Curtis Sharp, a one-time multi-million-dollar Lotto winner. And, as it turned out, the New Millionaires Club made its debut the same night of the biggest Lotto jackpot in New York State. But, since that lucky winner took a few days to claim his prize, guess who appeared on the cover of the *New York Post* the next morning: me, in my dollar-bill dress and dollar-sign earrings, along with model Curtis . . . quite a "Brill"iant media coup and stroke of luck!

Before I could catch my breath—I mean, the night after my show—I was a guest on "Late Night with David Letterman" and dressed the band. After that appearance, my designing talents became even more in demand. Custom orders came rolling in. Rock stars, especially, had a fondness for my hero-suits: drapey, tailored jackets over zooty trousers. Everyone from members of Duran Duran and Bruce Springsteen's E Street Band to Rod Stewart and the Rolling Stones were getting into my pants (and jackets and shirts). The cast of "Miami Vice" wore my clothes on camera, too. Think it was all fashion flash? Well, it was serious enough biz for *Manhattan Inc.* magazine to run a long feature article on me, cleverly titled "Blonde Prefers Gentlemen."

At its peak, Dianne Brill Menswear was nominated for the prestigious Cutty Sark Menswear Award. Yet after two strong seasons and an attempt to obtain an outside licensing deal, things fell apart financially for Dianne Brill Menswear. Okay. I lost my ass! (Literally, too—that's when I lost a lot of weight, but that's a chapter in itself!) But, like most business-mogul types, I bounced back, changed directions, and went on to pursue a number of challenging projects. I am a woman who can—and will—do anything I want. Acting. Modeling. Writing. Being! I discovered something wonderful that I could sell and that people would buy. My image. I began marketing *myselves*. Merchandising my me-ness in everything from window-display mannequins to fine German chocolates made in my shape. Babes, I know that when I really put my mind, heart, soul, back, and boobs into a project, it will work.

You can do the same.

THE
BIZ
OF IT ALL......

Which brings us to the purpose of the hot little book you now hold in your hands. It is my sincere objective to share, sister to sister, the wealth of my experience with all of you. I will give you, from my heart, the things I know most about and love: being a woman, a girl, and a babe in all kinds of situations.

The operative words in this book are "love," "fun," and "self." I will show you how you can have a great life by taking the best of your womanhood—strength, independence, intelligence, and self-esteem—and fusing it with the best of babedom—being the life of every party, enjoying your sexiness, adoring your men, and feeling beautiful.

CHAPTER 1

Meeting Great Guys

I am about to reveal to you guaranteed great guy-meeting methods. I know they work because I've tried them all and I've had amazing romantic results. So you're probably saying, "Sure, they work for *you*, Dianne: you could probably sneeze at a guy and have him on bended knee!" That's true—I can sneeze at a party and be offered a truckload of tissues, but only after getting dressed in just under six hours. What's important right now is that these strategies have been tested by my friends as well, and they, too, have had wild successes. What? You're surprised that I've shared my tactics with other women, not for profit but out of the goodness of my heart? Don't be. A true Sex Goddess is not a bitch (although she may play one on occasion). She adores women as much as men (usually in a different way, of course) and values the spiritual bond of Babedom.

Flirting environments are everywhere; everyone is flirting bait. Not that you're looking for "that love reaction" from everyone, but democracy in the initial stages of flirtation opens up every possibility. Of course you're discriminating, but there is Love God potential in every guy. English can be learned. Fu Manchu moustaches can be shaved off. Pecs can be developed and style can be acquired (or enforced, by you, Grande Dame of the fashion patrol). So many men. Yours for the taking. All you need are mystique, technique, and a few props (see Prop Till You Drop, just ahead) to establish your own Goddess Complex. Two points to keep in mind before you begin meeting more men than you know what to do with (don't worry; when you finish this book, you'll know):

1 It takes a secure, confident man to enjoy, without judgment, a direct approach from a woman. When shopping for a man, let him feel as though *he's* picked *you* out. Manipulation (why do you think they call it *man*-ipulation) is *not* like lingerie: don't even let a trace show.
2 No one wants it too easy—including you, babe. Men relish a touch of rejection as long as they know there's hope of eventual acceptance. So keep that balance between a bite and a kiss—tip it back and forth until he's dizzy with desire.

Designer Accessories and the Love Reaction

Listen carefully: You'll hear the name of your fashion accessory echoing from hallowed halls to street promenades. When you hear "Yo, Chanel!" "Get it, Gucci Girl," or even your name on a never-before-laid-your-eyes-on stranger GG's (great guy) lips, it's these accessories that make you approachable. Well, if "Get it, Gucci Girl!" isn't a gallant conversation starter to you, know this: You have the power to decide who merits your response, and you don't have to answer everybody's call.

THE BLANKET-FLIRT THEORY AND TECHNIQUE

Some of these flirting techniques may seem a bit flamboyant, but, in fact, he can't see your high IQ, sparkling wit, and warmth from across the room. By the same token, you can't see a guy's "hidden treasures" from a distance and will be attracted to the obvious—height, smile, shoulder width, whatever. So just assume that every man has something that you desire and employ an initial blanket flirt. Smiling to yourself as if you've just thought some whipped-cream-covered, secret sex thought is *mandatory*. Scanning a room quickly yet thoroughly and categorizing the men assembled is an essential skill that will become a reflex when you practice, practice, practice! Here's the formula:

1 Flirt—politely, with a warm smile and welcoming glance—with 100 percent of the men in a given room. Between 40 and 60 percent will counter-flirt to some degree.
2 Condense your flirt field-of-vision to the counter-flirters. Smile and glance at members of this group, but let your attention linger on each one a second longer. About 75 percent of these men will continue to counter-flirt (the rest will be waiting for their dates and won't go any further).
3 Narrow the group down to your lucky finalists. Find "the eyes" and lock in. Figure that a few will look away. The guys that remain are your best flirting options for the night.
4 Pick one and flirt with him directly, but discreetly, so as not to discourage the others. Flirt with him intensely but do not monopolize his time. Excuse yourself to check out all the other finalists (or repeat blanket-flirt process). Finally, crown the winner.

Here are some great places to meet great guys (from now on known as GGs) . . . and how to get them when you get there. So go on, get out there! Oh, by the way, first get dressed. What to wear? We'll cover that in detail later on, but my rule of thumb is when in doubt, overdress! Be sure your heels will be at least two inches higher than any other woman's in a given environment. Drench yourself in perfume. Also imperative: full makeup, tailored to the situation, setting, and lighting. Always. (The only exception is when you're dashing to the corner deli for your morning coffee; then, we all know, lipstick and sunglasses will

Prop Till You Drop

Clothing accessories: long gloves, long chiffon scarves, sunglasses, ornate lipstick cases, silk pocket squares, mirrored compacts, flirty hand-held clutch or handle purses.

Tootsie pops (keep three in your purse at all times: one for you, one for him, and one for the potential other him).

Borrowed adorable, fluffy dog (the pettable kind).

Camera (film is not necessary, unless you choose the tactic of actually taking a great guy's photo and promising to send it to him to ask for his address).

Walkman (tapes not necessary, so that when he asks you "What are you listening to?" your truthful reply will be: "You, handsome!").

Any small ethnic or antique objects (such as Greek worry beads, a priceless Fabergé egg, a Day-Glo zodiac keychain).

Fake nails.

Electronic gadgets that do something high-tech and useless.

Foreign magazine (French is best).

Dice.

Lavishly wrapped gift.

Small notebook and pen (take notes, doodle, sketch him).

Some kind of fashion accessory with a name on it, like a belt buckle or homeboy hat, shirt, pin, necklace, etc.

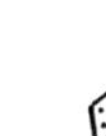

RAP
SONY

suffice.) Bear in mind that the following scenarios are only suggestions of what *might* happen—feel free to personalize and improvise as you go along! Now some situations may *look* like rejection—he flirts at first but doesn't follow through; who knows, he's married, in love, or acting the way someone else's boyfriend should when he sees a pretty girl. Just remember to take the "R" word in stride. Dignity and upness must be maintained. So if a GG doesn't see it your way this time, proceed to the next location.

Street

(Dress code: anything that makes you feel especially goddessy; makeup: same as for dress.) You can meet on the street at any time of day. The ideal times of year are when the seasons are first changing: The onset of winter makes a man look for a hibernating mate; in early spring, the fever rises; the first hint of summer is when things really get hot; and autumn is made for romantic strolling.

When out for a walk, don't spend all your time window shopping or admiring the architecture or you'll miss the potential Love God. The ultimate prop is a dog, but make it a cute dog, no matching pair of Doberman pinschers. But no matter when you're strollling, never take the short route home, because at home there are few chances to meet GGs. Check out the box ahead for some traffic-stopping walks.

Video Store

(Dress code: spicy-casual; makeup: clearly defined and well-blended to offset blinding lighting of store.) Most men rent vids for weekend viewing, so the best time to go is late afternoon/early evening on Friday or Saturday; or catch them on the return, Monday evening.

Scan for your man. Note the section he's perusing. If he's deliberating between *Bambi* and *Chitty Chitty Bang Bang*, you'll probably want to move on. Depending on your taste, you *may* want to pass on the guy who selects *Slasher Nuns Do Des Moines*.

Walk, Don't Run

Maybe you've noticed that all the gorgeous men are going in the wrong direction. Well, you can change that right now, depending upon which walk you choose. Here's the scene: You're walking toward each other and you make eye contact (when you get to be expert at this, you can make eye contact even if both you and GG are wearing dark shades). Keep walking but look over your shoulder to see if he's looking at you to see if you're looking at him. If he still appeals to you on second glance, 1) stop in your tracks and 2) keep looking with small smile (do not allow tongue to hang out of mouth). Most likely he will come to you, but it's okay to meet him halfway. You can even take the first step. So now you're face to face. If he's still quiet, look at him with a slightly confused expression as if he looks familiar. Do *not* say: "Don't I know you?" Instead ask: "Who are you?" One perfect line, three ways to say it. Put the accent on whichever word feels right: *Who* are you? Who *are* you? Who are *you*?

One walk is worth a thousand words! Study the struts of your idols and incorporate their step-styles with your own.

Walk Into Your Grand Entrances: Deep breath (hold it), chin up, smile on. Pause at the doorway and look through the crowd. Carry yourself as tall as possible (no hunching or slouching). Put one hand at your hip (a gesture that demands plenty of space) and take the room with sweeping, smooth steps.

Best Exits: Pretend that you're walking an imaginary line. This is a little knock-kneed from the front but unbeatable from behind.

Double Takes: Stop in your tracks, bend your right knee seductively forward, and then turn your head with an upward motion, swinging tresses proudly.

Silky Strides: While stocking-legged, softly glaze your calves together and let them touch for a second with each long stride you take.

For Wiggle Enhancement: Follow in the steps of Marilyn Monroe and have the shoemaker file down one of your heels by a quarter of an inch.

Beach and Boudoir: Whenever barefoot, tiptoe!

Okay, you see he's made a selection. Let's say *Pillow Talk* with Doris Day and Rock Hudson. (And you know your video store only carries one copy of each film.) Purr to the clerk behind the counter: "I simply *must* see *Pillow Talk* tonight!"

Either of two extremes will occur: He insists you take the tape, or insists that you watch it together at his/your place. Do neither! Instead, give away the ending (if you don't know it just say they live happily ever after). Disappointment will register on his face. Apologize for ruining his movie plans for the night and inquire if there's any way you might make it up to him. Like maybe you could treat him to a matinee!

Dry Cleaners

(Dress code: dry-clean-only fine fabric, such as cashmere; makeup: sophisticasual.) Peak time is Saturday in the late afternoon/early evening, when your man won't be picking up boring business suits but something expensive and fun.

You scope out a GG—let's say he's having the sleeve of a leather jacket lengthened. Upon receiving your clothes, you tell the dry cleaner that something is missing—a scarf is always good, it's small and easy to misplace. Murmur politely at first and become increasingly insistent (but always sexy—never whine!). This will get GG to take notice of you (if he hasn't already). Soon as he turns to you, forget *completely* about your cherished lost scarf and tell GG: "You look gorgeous in that jacket." This will embarrass him, make him vulnerable. Accent your statement with a sidelong glance and bad-girl smile, then quickly shift back to the matter of the missing scarf. Yet, important as the item is to you, you simply can't concentrate in GG's presence; you shift your attention back to him once more and say, in your best "Biker Barbie" voice: "I just love bikes. Got one to go with that jacket?" The question as come-on is foolproof; he should respond with: "Sure. Would you like to go for a ride?" You roar off into the sunset, your "Biker Barbie" scarf, which has been around your neck all along, blowing in the breeze.

Markets

(Dress code: richness; makeup: absolute perfection, with impeccably manicured nails.) You're in the market for a man, not salad fixings! It's vital to come off as if you can't boil water. Even if you can out-soufflé the chefs of Paris, you can always impress him with your cuisine artistry after the romance has taken off; in the beginning you want to be taken out (and well).

Supermarket (ten-items-or-less line): GGs don't clip coupons or stock up on red-dot specials; they keep very little in their refrigerators (the best have only champagne and condiments). Men go to the supermarket after work on weekdays or on Saturday. Get in line behind him and ask him to please hold your place, as if you've forgotten something. Come back obviously empty-handed. Thank him warmly and say: "Darn, they're all out of espresso and I'm really in the mood . . . for some." At which point he will whisk you away to the nearest café.

Gourmet Shop: Drop in for some sun-dried tomatoes and smoked buffalo mozzarella in the early evening on Thursday, when Love Gods will be shopping for weekend ambrosia. Be aware that while you'll see many GGs in delicacy boutiques, a percentage of them have gourmet tastes for others of the male persuasion. Ask him about an odd item in his basket. If he says, "Girlfriend, it's *divine* overness! And surprisingly low in calories," chat with him a moment and exchange diet tips, then head to the highly caloric chocolate section. Chances are good that the GG who overindulges in chocolate will want to overindulge in you.

Twenty-Four-Hour Fruit Stand: Go way past the witching hour (three A.M. is peak) to meet a dashing night person. Fondle the fruits and vegetables. Stick to things like melons but eschew the cucumbers—a man could get easily intimidated and flustered when you're holding one of those huge green missiles. Inquire if he knows how to tell when something is ripe.

Newsstands

(Dress code: always a dress, somewhat—but not too—snug and skimpy with a simple high heel; makeup: newsworthy.) These hotbeds of activity could score you more than just the morning headlines! Hit the newsstand in a nearby office building early morning (before the hectic nine o'clock rush). For the general newsstand, go at off-hours, late afternoon, or three in the morning. My personal favorite, the hotel kiosk (the best place to meet a man in a hotel; Sex Goddesses do not prowl lobbies!), is also best in the early A.M.; even if you're on vacation, set your travel alarm or request a wake-up call.

Browse in a leisurely manner (men are frisky, sharp, and alert in the morning and will be taken with a woman who has the time to peruse at her own pace). Chuckle throatily over a picture to intrigue him, then give him a peek as if you're sharing a secret. This minor conspiracy you form by including him in your little joke gives him the freedom—in a friendly way—to approach you. A word to the wise: Don't embarrass him while he's leafing through porno: while you may not go for it yourself, to a man porno is sacred.

Elevator

(Dress code: sensuous-important; makeup: kissable.) The elevator is a great old standby. Go when lunch hour is just beginning or at day's end (it is more difficult to get his eye when he's trying to figure out a novel excuse for being late!).

Go to the back of the elevator, a power position that gives you a view of everyone. Scan. Elevators are such a crossroads, you can strike up a conversation about anything. The easiest ice-breaker of all: simply ask GG to please push your floor button.

Okay, you've got to be a pretty fast worker to pull this off in one ride (or else it's a *really* tall building!). You may, however, notice the same GG in your elevator on several occasions; try forming an elevator relationship over a number of rides. Become familiar with each other, via nods and smiles, and work up to asking, "Do you work in this building?"

Vehicles

(Cars, taxis, limos, and planes) (Dress code: Anything that spotlights you from the waist up—for the "window line" of your vehicle—and from the waist down—for your grand, leggy exits; makeup: tailored to where you're going but striking enough to keep their eyes on you, not your hood ornament(!); props: a map of any town, also, something eye-catching: A frisky L.A. friend of mine always wears one perfect elbow-length white glove on her left arm—to keep from getting sunburned—or so she says).

Cars: You'll gain new appreciation for traffic jams once you master "intercar communications." I was so involved with car games, my license was revoked (I'll be eligible for one again sometime in the late 1990s). With car cruising, it's only appropriate that *you* make the first move (disregard anyone who honks, beeps, or shouts "nice headlights!" in your direction). Also be aware that the cliché expensive cars often carry men who don't make the greatest first impression—but are still worth pursuing as they may have something under the hood. Keep glancing at the driver of your choice. If he changes lanes, do the same to keep him in your sights (preferably with him on the driver's side). Sidle your car up next to his, rev the engine, and—ignoring the gridlock—ask him, "Wanna race?"

Taxis: Sharing a taxi—at your suggestion—is never risky because you can always hop out at a traffic light. You spy a GG waiting at the same corner as you are. It doesn't matter who was there first. Ask him if he's going uptown (of course he is, he's facing that direction). Ask him if he'd like to share a cab (naturally he says yes). Sitting together in such proximity should elicit memories of teenage backseat romance for both of you. The simplest way to start a conversation is to ask where he's headed. If you're more adventurous tell him that your first kiss just happened to take place in the back seat of a yellow car.

Planes: Ever notice how gender differences manifest themselves on long airplane flights? The men are constantly pacing the length of the plane while the women are nesting in their seats. I say, join the men: walk the aisles and watch things *really* take off. Scan at the gate before boarding. It doesn't matter where you're supposed to sit, you can always move. Walk slowly to the farthest bathroom and catch his eye on your way. Should the plane hit some turbulence, be sure to go with the ride, not against it, to maintain a graceful sashay. Take an empty seat near him and monitor his activities, waiting for the opportune moment when he joins his fellow male pacers. In the meantime, be sure to keep that pretty stewardess *very* busy bringing you drinks, pillows, etc., so she won't be able to attend to *your* GG. When he gets up, you go toward him so you'll meet up face-to-face in the narrow aisle. You needn't wait for an air pocket to pitch you into his arms; simply ask him if he has dinner plans for this flight.

Limos: So that you shouldn't waste the luxury of a limousine, this exit is guaranteed to cause at least one explosive collision! When getting out of the limo, lean forward and breathe in deeply. Pretend to have lost something—let's say a diamond earring. Then, upon finding it on your ear, after half the pedestrians (all men!) have desperately combed the ground for it, squeal with laughter. Next, arms at your sides, pushing in together, let your forearms cross underneath the boobs creating your noncompromising cleavage. With the right index finger posed seductively on one corner of your lower lip, say, wide-eyed: "Oh, silly me! Here it is." Now *back* out of the crowd, smiling triumphantly, and wiggle into the restaurant. Breathe *out*. Great! Your target(s) will follow you helplessly into the restaurant.

Bars, Clubs, and Parties

These are the most obvious GG meeting grounds. You know this, babes! And what you don't know, I'll discuss in detail in the chapter "How to Be the Queen of the Night Every Night." So all I'll say now is that these environments populated with a huge "bevy of boys" can be tricky—there's pressure, dark lighting, loud music, a lot of distractions. That means you need an extra bit of good-humored ammunition, flirt-wise. It's the Danilo Wink and it will not fail you (see box ahead).

Trendy Restaurant

(Dress code: drop-dead devastating glam-gal gorgeous; makeup: femme fatale formidable, smoldery, and sultry.) Later hours (GGs tend to prefer supper to dinner) when the restaurant will be crowded but not crammed are best. Monday through Thursday in metropolitan areas, Friday and Saturday in suburbs, never on Sunday (a universal family and couples' time).

Prop properly! A wrapped birthday present with lots of bows (men love to untie those pretty ribbons) is a real conversation-starter; he can approach and ask: "Is it your birthday?" A pair of long gloves is good: carry one, put it on, take it off, play with it. Sunglasses are effective: with one elegant finger extended, push shades down, from top of rim peer at him. A pretty compact comes in handy—you can use the mirror to check out the GGs behind you. Indispensible: overly perfumed, sheer chiffon scarves, a long one at your neck or at your purse or neck to play with and a small one for the "Pocket Square Exchange" (details ahead).

It's best to go to a place you've been to before; it's always good to know the maitre d'. Your party should be composed of a few lively people who adore you. There should be at least one man in the group who is obviously not your date to add interest to your group and create an opening for another man to join.

The Danilo Wink

This subtle but potent technique was passed along to me by one of the most successful flirts I know (next to me, of course): the international superstar hair stylist Danilo Dixon. It says it all . . . without making a sound. This very special wink takes practice—a lot. The secret is not in the eye but in the mouth and eye in perfect sync, signaling your intentions across the room.

Look in a mirror, beautiful. In almost slow-motion speed, close your right eye, as in a classical wink. Simultaneously make an almost imperceptible, gentle pout, leading with the right side of your mouth. Practice repeatedly until you get it. Lips should quiver into a pucker like the beginning of a "why" sound. Your face should not scrunch up as if a snowflake had landed above your lip. Do not sneer. This is one of the few times in life when less really is more. Caution: The mood of this wink demands soft lighting, do it in the dark or near-dark; avoid office fluoresence or direct sunlight.

P.S.: If you can't wink just one eye, do as celebrated Sex Goddess Jayne Mansfield did: quickly close and open both eyes at once and smile while you pout for more winklike authenticity.

Scan immediately upon entering the restaurant: Do the bar first, then take your first silky stride to the ladies room to canvass the area thoroughly. There he is, standing by the bar—that GG who takes your breath away.

Be sure to be seated close to the GG of your choice (one good reason to know the maitre d'). He must be within eyeshot or earshot. Do not sit next to the man in your party. Angle your body slightly so you're perched near the edge of the chair, three fourths of your body turned toward the GG of your choice. Your face should be directed at your group of mixed friends, but in this position it will be easy for you to turn toward him and give him a three-quarter glimpse of your ravishing visage. I don't know why, but a three-quarter face is always the most flattering presentation. It may be to your advantage if the man in your party loves men the same way you do, as he will understand the sitch and not ask loudly: "Why aren't you facing the table, Mona?"

Always drink from a long-stemmed glass (even if it's Tab). Play with your props. Give GG a look and hold it, but only while engaged in sparkling conversation with your table. He may think you're talking to him but won't be sure. He might look away. Don't panic. He knows you're there. Repeat a few minutes later, but this time pause mid-sentence and give him that cat-who-got-the-cream smile. As soon as he reacts (and he will) with a smile or hopeful expression, turn around and return to the conversation.

He's embarrassed now and pretends to be engrossed in his fennel salad. Time for trip number two to the ladies room. But first, do the "Knife Trick" (see box ahead).

Pass his table and look back over one shoulder. Practice this pose at home, perhaps throwing in a hair flip or amused/surprised expression; be sure it looks natural (so rehearse!). Quick primp-stop—don't take too long in the ladies room but do take a circuitous route back to your table to make sure you haven't missed a better guy seated elsewhere. If

THE KNIFE TRICK

Don't worry, it's nothing dangerous. The Knife Trick should be practiced throughout the meal to avoid lipstick on the teeth or the dreaded spinach smile (definitely not seductive). Be sure to order a knife wherever you are (even in a Japanese restaurant or pizzeria!).

To check your look during dinner, discreetly tilt your knife up toward you. Pretend to laugh slightly at something someone said and look at your reflection. No spinach, no lipstick, a triumph!

Doin' the knife trick with my man in London.

Fear not should your terribly perceptive dinner companion catch you performing the Knife Trick. Pretend that you did it obviously so that he'd notice, then raise the knife so that both of you are reflected and say: "Don't we make a gorgeous couple?"

you have, perform the Pocket Square Exchange (see box opposite), quickly, with him.

As you pass his table, nod in recognition or, better yet, raise one eyebrow (both brows if you can't do just one). Sit down ever so slowly and re-engage in your table's banter.

Finally it's time to get him involved. As if he's been part of your group all evening, face him and direct a question to him. Listen intently to his answer, any answer, then offer an important counterquestion. As he's answering, pretend you can't hear him by whispering: "I can't hear you." Bingo! He's at your table. He'll repeat himself. Say, in an even lower whisper, "I can't hear you." He'll move in even closer. Then ask him a lot of questions about himself. Do not talk about yourself. He will be certain to say: "You're really an interesting girl. When can I see you again?"

You will find this the most satisfying meal you never ate!

The Pocket Square Exchange

This is a required battle plan for every perfume-packing member of the Brill Babe Brigade. It's an irresistible and unique little manuever that will guarantee a second meeting with a selected Love God.

If you're wearing a jacket, tuck a heavily scented square of fine chiffon into the breast pocket; if not, keep the scarf in your purse. While at the bar in a restaurant (or any similar situation: at a party, at a club, etc.), approach him and inhale, exchange your pocket square for his, spending a bit of time arranging it attractively in his jacket. (If he doesn't have a square in his pocket, put yours in his and immediately walk away, but stay within sight.) The perfume on your scarf will seduce his senses while everything is on the up-and-up and perfectly proper. From across the room, look at him and touch the square you "borrowed" repeatedly as if you're very fond of it. He will *have to* approach you; don't you approach him—you've already made the first move. Remark how your scarf complements his suit much better than the one you borrowed (or vice versa, his goes better with your outfit). Chat for a while. If you don't find him fun, re-exchange pocket squares; if he's all you thought he'd be, say, "I'll return this the next time we meet!"

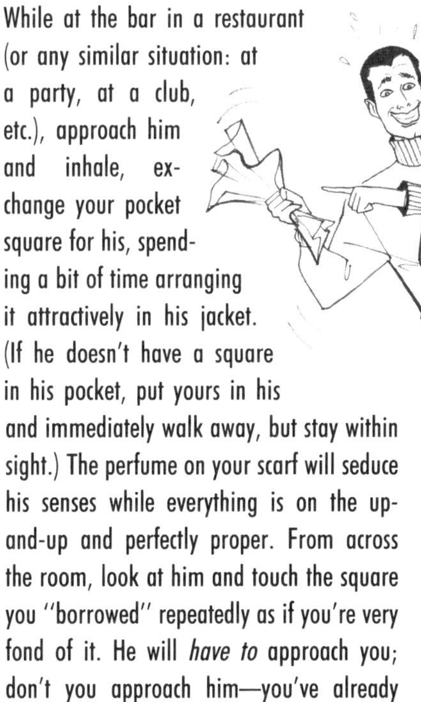

CHAPTER 2

Dating, Romancing, and Seducing

Too many men? No such thing, doll, when there's so much love sampling to be done. Have a harem of hims, those datable delights waiting for their hot little love angel: *vous*. Hmmm. At its finest, monogamy takes you to the highest heights, and eventually you will find that sole soul mate . . . but take it slow. Procrastination is key when you're looking for love-lasting. Date till you *drop*! Close your eyes . . . pick one (okay, leave your eyes open and pick one!). Be ambitious for love while holding out on changing the monograms on your new towels after his first call. Save the "Is-he-going-to-be-the-one" mind chant for later, like on the fifth call. This way, you can make the right choice after the fab old days of boy scouting.

There are so many types of men, yours for the dating! Which is your type? Did you say "all"? Good answer! Be versatile! Be democratic! Different kinds of men will fill a variety of slots on your social calendar. Check out the chart below to help you organize your guys:

RATE-A-DATE

Man/Description	Function
Momentary Madness Man: He's all wrong, but at the moment, he's just right.	Instant gratification.
The Stash Babe: An ex or almost lover with whom you have some unresolved romantic past.	Rescue . . . from whatever state you're in. He's your underdog hero.
Po'-Boy: His pockets may be empty but his trousers are full.	To invite himself to your place, where he'll whip up a gourmet meal from whatever's in *your* fridge, then watch videos on *your* VCR while massaging your sweet feet.
Rich-Boy: He won't buy you a tiara—only a large, glittering crown will do.	This is the easiest, go-anywhere, do-anything guy. Accept all grandiose gifts with enthusiasm—never feel guilty, because, to paraphrase Marilyn Monroe, a man being rich is like a girl being pretty.
The Man Who Loves Women Too Much: When he moans, "You're the only one for me, Cymbellina . . . ," you can't help but wonder how many other Cymbellinas have heard his same murmurings.	A flash date—perfect to escort you to any high-profile event because he owns his own tux and will take it in stride if you flirt shamelessly with every other man in attendance.

Man/Description	**Function**
The "Your Face Here" Guy: He looks like or reminds you of the "the one that got away."	He's a nonnutritive sweetener, a real sugar substitute. He fills a void temporarily. Go easy on him.
The Rebel And The Out-Of-Towner: You know you can't hold him but he dares you to try.	Brief, intense, romantic, magical love story; a try-on preparation for the real thing.
Sir Right: You love his long-comings and even like his short-comings.	The right guy at the right time.

The bad date does not exist. Believe me, I've been on all kinds, and I've discovered that all are love experiments, learning experiences (even if what you learn is what you *don't* want), and good dating practice. I've survived the kinds of dates a lot of you babes probably dread.

There was the blind date. It was, of course, set up by my mother. Everybody's mother has a friend who has a son that's just perfect for you. His name was Butch and it was my job to keep him occupied for an entire afternoon while his Mumsie prepared a surprise birthday party for him. It was sort of a moral obligation—the birthday pressure was more than I could withstand, so I said okay.

We took my family's sailboat-for-two to the beach, and it was absolutely my Sunfish Trip of Torment. Butch was straight, honorable, and a college man—everything that a teenage beach bunny (me) doesn't want! He didn't even have a tan. I kept trying to tip the boat over while telling shark stories. He seemed undaunted, so I pulled the "I've-got-to-go-to-the-bathroom" routine, and, despite the fact that there was a whole ocean around us, I insisted we sail to the facilities on shore. Seventeen times. Of course, on shore, where all the cute GGs were hanging. I flirted, unabashed, hoping someone would rescue me, but no lifeguard came to my aid as Butch kept pulling me out to sea, again and again.

The party was due to start at 5:00 P.M. I looked at my waterproof watch. It was 3:30. An hour later, I looked again. It was 3:32. I could take it no longer and feigned *mal de mer*. It was supposed to be a surprise party. Well, the surprise was on them. When we arrived at his house, my best girlfriend—who was invited to give me emergency cool-to-cool resuscitation—took one look at Butch and fell genuinely in love with him.

What, you're no doubt wondering, did I learn from this? That what looks like junk to you is a hunk to someone else. Boys can—and should—be recycled. So don't ditch him, introduce him.

Then there was my personal-ad date experience. . . . The doorbell rang. It was my bosom buddy Janis. "You're not going to believe it," she said, handing me a copy of *New York* magazine, opened to the personals section. There it was, circled in Fuchsia Shock lipstick:

Dianne Brill lookalike wanted—by wealthy dynamic duality, cultivated British man, big blue eyes, needing one special voluptuous woman. NYM A885.

Naturally, I had to go . . . but I wanted to play it as a lookalike, and I made myself a solemn vow that I would not reveal my true identity. First I had my building's super do photography duty and take some Polaroids of me. Then I wrote a charming note, enclosed the snaps, and, in my swirliest, girliest handwriting, signed my pseudonym: Sabina Kendall. He called in due course and we arranged to meet at a tearoom.

I didn't have to wear a red carnation—he knew me when he saw me. He looked atypically English, except for the odd and probably once-

The photo I sent to my personal ad date: me as Sabina Kendall.

Hello,

I'm Sabina, I read your ad in N.Y. Mag, and am happy to say that I could be Ms. Brill's twin or so everyone tells me.

I love England and especially Englishmen. Could we meet for tea?

Please call me and ask for Sabina Kendall. It would be great to get together as soon as possible.

Hoping to see you soon,

XOXO Sabina.

trendy, white silk (in winter!) Armani jacket. We chatted over tea and scones, and after a while he said: "You certainly do look quite a bit like Dianne Brill!" I thanked him for the compliment. "But," he continued, "I met a lady who could be her twin. So I hope you'll understand . . ." he started to stammer, so I patted his passé jacket reassuringly and thanked him for a lovely afternoon. My God! *I* was dumped for not being Dianne Brill enough! I left feeling flattered by his third-person compliments, but I must admit, a little sad: His once-trendy white silk Armani jacket had started to grow on me.

So you see what I mean when I say: From the weird to the wild to the wonderful, all dates are worthwhile. Especially when you know the rules. You make your own rules, so they're easy to remember, and, fortunately, most dating rules are as elastic as a new garter belt—you can stretch them to suit the situation. Say you find yourself trembling with desire fifteen seconds after meeting a GG and feel the time is right to go to bed with him. Maybe the time *is* right—if he's a rebel or you're feeling like a rebellette with condoms in tow. But know this: If you think this GG could be Sir Right, sex after fifteen seconds could narrow your chances of finding out.

Let's face it: Men come to love the one they are sexually attracted to while women get more and more sexually attracted to the one they love. Also, men want to want. There's a dichotomy at work: They will try to bed you quickly, but at the same time want to feel that they've worked hard to win you. What's crucial is to make him totter off the edge into pure amour, and each date brings him closer to the brink.

Most likely, he'll try his best to bed you by the third date, because men still abide by the Third Date Rule (TDR). That's why you have to resist. If he breaks the TDR for you (in other words, he asks you out again despite no third-date love action), then you know that you've built a foundation of trust. When you finally do wake up in his bed, you'll *belong* there.

There's another important reason why you must lust till you're ready to bust. You know he wants you. (Look him in his eyes: Pupil dilation? Sort of pulsing, fevered stare? Yep! You've got him!) But you need the time to find out if *you* really do want *him*. Float in the fun of being wined and dined while you decide. Remember, anything worth having is worth waiting for—and worth dating for.

Also, the longer you wait, the more powerful you become. Power is everything in Datesville, doll. No man wants a wimpy woman, the way no woman wants a mushy man. Bear in mind the difference between *wanting* him (oh, yeah!) and *needing* him (never, never—at least not in the beginning!). He wants you to challenge him, inspire him; yes, he wants to be taunted, even tricked. Men love to be hungry, and only a truly powerful, proud, and sensuously endowed woman knows how to give him a tiny taste of what's ahead, just enough to make him come back for more, more, more!

Power protects your tender heart—femme fatales are not infallible. While I definitely endorse risk-taking—dating all kinds of guys—I think its a good idea to arrest heartbreak. Give too much too soon and it's an open invitation for the man to pounce your wildly beating passion-pumper. And so, in summation, when you're ambitious for love, *procrastination* is key.

After the fourth encounter with your GG, you are no longer simply dating. You have—drumroll, please—a budding relationship. Ah, but the secret to getting to that point is to be absolute dating dynamite. Each time you see him, and every flirty, frisky phone call in between, is an opportunity to steal a piece of his heart. Dates are much more than a chance to show off your new Mugler or Alaia suit or practice your exquisite table manners. Dates are where you make him your own. Each date is a big seduction number. Arouse. Incite. Carouse. Delight. All towards a glorious goal! To be sure you reach that goal, I'll take you through, step by step, those vital first four dates.

♥ THE FIRST DATE

Finally! He called! (You met Saturday night and it's only Tuesday, but you were sitting by the phone chipping the polish off your nails and worrying that he had lost your number or that maybe your 4s look like 9s). Hah! Of course, he called!

The first date is the most important because it sets the stage for all the rest. It's also the one you're both most nervous about.

Avoid first-date fumbles by going to the right place. It's always a good sign that this guy is a true GG when he has a plan: He made the reservation, got tickets to some glamorous event, is on the guest list for the club, picked out a couple of movie choices, etc. Surely you know that this won't make the Guiness Book of Great Dates if he arrives at your door, shlumpily attired, and mumbles, "So, whaddya wanna do tonight?"

The majority of men, however, take a middle-ground approach and ask in advance how you'd like to spend the evening. Going out for dinner is usually a good first date: It's intimate, doesn't have to be expensive, and allows for conversation. But there are some guidelines. Most important: Pick a restaurant with gentle lighting (if there's a little candle on your table, inconspicuously push it away from your face, as underlighting will give the appearance of a horror movie extra!). It's to your advantage to select a place you've been to before and like—the waiters will know you and treat you well. However, skip the place where all the waiters know your phone number. Also avoid overcrowded, overnoisy, or overtrendy spots. Too much of "Hey, Dianne, you look gorgeous—is this Johnny?" when your date's name is Christophe can kill the magic of the moment. Pay attention to cuisine—pass on Mexican (beans-on-the-breath) and Indian (those curried sweats!).

Okay, now you're out together. What are you going to talk about? Avoid boring stuff like what he does for a living (even if you're after his money, a good gold-digger is always gracious and learns his tax bracket through more subtle means!). In the early stages of date-chat, form the perfect conspiracy: just you two on one side and everyone else on the other side. For instance, say to him: "What if time stood still right now like in a 'Twilight Zone' episode, and you and I were the only ones who could move around this room freely. What would you do first? A: Unzip all the ladies' skirts? B: Raid the dessert cart? C: Commit a criminal act, like bringing me those diamond earrings off the blonde sitting at the table behind us?" (If he's a true GG, he'll pick C.)

This game is a great little ice-breaker. As the date goes on, steer the conversation so it gets more personal and stick to the most important subject: *him.* Ask plenty of questions. Make them romantic, intimate, personal, and throw in a few focused compliments. Here are a few examples: Tell me a secret; you look like a man with a lot of secrets. Talk about the ocean on a dark, warm night when the waves *swell* and *crash*, *swell* and *crash*, like before a storm, the sky turning purple and the foam lush against the shore . . . then that calm happens . . . and you know the world is just going to . . . open . . . up! Then, sipping daintily from your drink, ask him: "Have you ever been in a storm? Hurricane? Tornado? What did it look like? How did it make you feel?" Your queries should be provocative and intriguing, and shouldn't have a yes-no answer.

Exploit the cultural differences between you. Pick up on words or phrases he uses that hint at where he comes from. Ask him to explain what they mean. Remark on how interesting they are, or how his accent or tone of his voice has a magnetic effect on you. Always use your questions and respond in ways that are flourishing with flattery.

Complimenting your date is key. I don't think *anyone* can get enough compliments, especially a man, so flatter up! *How* you flatter matters. He wants it to be sincere. You don't want him to say: "I bet you say that to all the boys!" It's not only what you say but how you say it—the way you slow down and lower your voice to emphasize key words. Pout when you speak. Start thinking in italics! Choose your words carefully: Half a foot always sounds bigger and better than six inches.

Don't underestimate the intensity of your gaze, the way you look into his eyes when you deliver a compliment. Skip the obvious. Don't say: "Nice tie." Say: "It's amazing how the little flecks of amber in your eyes glitter in this light." Pick up on his unique characteristics—the way he curls one side of his mouth when he smiles or wrinkles his forehead when he's concentrating—and point them out.

Of course, with all you complimenting of him, he'll be compelled to return flattery favors. You must be able to accept a compliment properly. It's the silly girl who, when a man says, "You're beautiful," replies with a "No, I'm not, really. My eyes are too close together, my nose is half a millimeter too long, the mole on my cheek really would look better by my lower lip . . ." Such a list of your flaws will make any GG uncomfortable—and may make him look at you in a new (ghastly!) light. The best way to receive a compliment is to pause to absorb it and let it warm you. Then smile an easy, genuine smile, and all you have to say is thank you.

What else can you talk about besides each other? Talk about beauty in all its forms, specifically, a child you met, a sunset you watched, a yellow moon you saw.

You may be wondering whether there's a difference between conversation and a trade-off of "lines." I think there is, because conversation is spontaneous and lines are rehearsed—but that's not to say that lines don't serve a good purpose. Some lines have been overused and abused. The best lines are original and pertain to you specifically, like the one John Wayne gave Maureen O'Hara: "Between your red hair and your green eyes, I don't know whether to stop or to go." By the way, he went! Bear in mind: *Men will say anything in their boyish exuberance to get laid!*

Lines that make your head spin: "You're a mythical statue yet so warm, so real—in you, I have the best of worlds. You're my fantasy; my Venus and my nemesis. It doesn't matter what you wear tonight: not a single stitch, not a thread, could make you more beautiful than you are to me right now."

Lines to give you an instant headache: "The way you smoke that cigarette makes me jealous. I'm a one-woman man . . . one woman at a time. I'm a man and I know what a man wants and this man wants to see you in a pair of them nice, tight Sergio Valentes! It doesn't matter what you wear tonight—you won't be wearing it for long, anyway, Thunderbutt."

Sometimes actions speak louder than words, lovergirl! The way you move, sit, toy with your props, look at him, etc., send out powerful signals. Be conscious of your behavior. A truly GG I know told me about a girl he took out—only once—because even though he was doing most of the talking, he kept catching her admiring herself in the mirror behind him. Always be aware of what you're doing on a date—and the effect it has on him.

Sexy little things mean a lot: for instance, raising your eyebrow (always full of suggestion, maybe seduction) or tossing your hair (sexy free-spiritedness). Touch yourself—no, not there! Everyplace else. Stroke your fingers across your soft cheek; trace a slow figure eight against your knee; pretend to adjust your belt or blouse while pulling your shoulders back. By touching yourself you subliminally create the need in him to touch you. It's also nice to touch him while you chat, to help you make your point and reinforce your interest. Just let your fingers graze his arm or rest on his hand—it really breaks down barriers.

There will probably be some lapses in conversation that may make you and him feel awkward. Try the Hairbrush Trick (see box ahead) and

THE HAIRBRUSH TRICK

Take your hairbrush from your purse and "accidentally" drop it on the floor of the car. Keep it hidden by your feet but reach down and feel around for it while looking up at him. You can't find it, so you say, "Oops! Maybe I'm sitting on it." Raise your derriere and feel around for it. Still no luck! When you stop for a traffic light, ask him to please help you. Together, you feel around, looking for it. Magically the brush appears! Thank him for his help, then drop the brush again in front of him. Laugh and say, "Oops, lost again!"

use your imagination to invent other games to fill the silence with flirtatious fun!

So you've had a lovely time and now comes the moment of truth: the first good night kiss, which is very important. Remember, the eyes may be the window of the soul but the mouth is the window of the heart. If you never, ever want to see this man's face again, give him a polite wave good-bye, and exit quickly! Kissless.

However, if there's any potential whatsoever, your kiss must be full of promise. Prepare for the goodnight kiss half an hour before. Sip some wine or water, then, when he's not looking, take a shot of breath spray (if you don't have an opportunity to do this, offer him a breath mint and take one for yourself). It's essential to do this fifteen minutes before the kiss, because he doesn't want to taste that golden drop of retsin, he wants to taste your mouth.

While he's driving you home, lean forward into his rearview mirror (forget the one in the visor on your side!) Stare at your lips; then adjust the corners of your mouth for stray lipstick. Don't do any obvious licking or pouting. Finally, move your gaze and give him a sidelong glance, then sit back down, just slightly closer to him than before. (If you're in a cab, compensate by looking in your compact.)

At your door, tell him you had a lovely time *with him.* Put your eyes to the floor and feign a coy moment, then look up at him. You must let *him* kiss *you*, and this signals an invitation for him to snuggle on your pillowlips. Let the tension build: Break eye contact (look at his mouth instead of his eyes) and feel him without touching him—the time when you're standing close together and thinking about kissing is incredibly sexy. Draw this out as long as you can, then look into his eyes again and accept his kiss. I'm not going to tell you how to kiss—you know that. I'll just say this: Be as wanton as you want as long as you still hold the reins and can leave this stallion stomping in *his* stable, not yours.

Phonetiquette for Between Dates One and Two

We all know how much phone calls from a man mean. Like when Alberto calls you from Rome three times in a half-hour period. You think, "He called me three times today!"; you don't think, "Well, we got disconnected twice." So even though you may be tempted to reach for the phone the minute a date drops you off . . . don't touch that dial. It's usually better for him to call you first, to thank you for your scintillating company.

Perhaps you've been on phone patrol since you got home from the date—but should you let him know you've been holding your breath for his call? The best way to react to his first follow-up phone call is with warmth—maybe even a touch of heat. Never chilly (play it too cool and you're the fool!) or overly torrid.

KISSING AND TELLING

How to tell from one kiss if he's maybe not right for you:

You kiss him—and you don't like the way he tastes. Then hug him and sniff the place just behind his ear—and you don't like his smell. Unless he's not a bather or is extremely overcologned, chances are your sexual chemistry, your compatibility, is not there . . . or at least not yet. Don't immediately write this guy off, but take the signal for what it's worth.

It may just happen that you miss his call. He'll leave a message on your machine, and whether he asks you out or not, call him back! True, you may get into a game of message tag, but that can be fun. When you leave him a message, you must sound friendly and in a good mood. The message must be super short and give him the impression that you have a secret he's dying to discover. Never leave a message that says, "Hi, it's me!" unless you have been previously engaged or married to this man! Never call and hang up more than once—he'll get the message that it's you. Better to leave a message in a foreign accent.

Of course, you'll never know when exactly he'll call you back, so be sure to Telepurr every time you pick up the phone (see box).

♥ THE SECOND DATE

What is the plan of action here? This is the date where you hook the guy you're crazy about or give a second chance to a guy you're not sure of. Here's when you start reading into the conversation and do a little discreet digging. Many women make the mistake of overanalyzing what men say. Usually, when he says "hello" he means hello. However, a bit of analysis is okay. Consult the chart below for general interpretations.

TRANSLATING SECOND DATESPEAK

What He Says	What He Means
Do you have a boyfriend?	I have a girlfriend.
Oh, your CD player needs to be hooked up?	Finally, I'll be alone with her in her apartment!
Do you always wear your hair up?	I wish she'd wear her hair loose.
Are those new shoes?	I hope she bought those sexy stilettos exclusively for me
Do you have an alarm clock?	Can we get tangled together in your sheets tonight?

Telepurr

When you hear the phone ring, immediately hold your breath. Let it ring two or three times (depending on your particular lung capacity). Then lift the receiver and very slowly exhale and smile (he can hear your expression). Press your lips against the mouthpiece and, slow and low, so that your voice runs up his loins, say the word: "Hellllooooooo."

After you say "Hellllooooooo," tell him it's great to hear his voice. Always encourage the first-time caller. Give him the impression that you're terribly busy—but that nothing is more important right now than talking to him. This is where you can use your call-waiting to its best advantage (every Sex Goddess must have this service!). Men always have to believe that somebody else wants you; it makes them want you more. But even if no calls happen to come in while you're speaking to him, pretend you're getting beeped twice during the course of the conversation. At the first interruption say, "Oh, I'm getting another call," but ignore it until you get (or pretend to get) a second beep. Then ask him an intimate question, but before he can respond, say, "I've got to take this call; I'll be right back, I promise!" Any other interruptions (real or imaginary) should be ignored—let him know you've got the call but that you don't want to stop talking to him. Make sure you sound upbeat and positive throughout the call to set up a secure base for him to ask you for another date. If he doesn't, it's just because he's intimidated, so you've got the freedom to say, "I want to see your fabulous face!" Then take charge, doll, and say, "Let's go to—insert your favorite date place here—Thursday night. Can you make it?" You know he wants to *make it* with you!

Sometimes you'll decide, alas, after a second date, that this fellow is simply not for you at this time. However, it's vital that you never burn your bridges—you never know when he might have a great party to invite you to or a gorgeous cousin to introduce you to! It's imperative to let a guy down easy. Here are some rules for a Dump-a-Date:

1 Never leave your hands empty—so he won't try to hold them. Constantly play with your bracelets, rings, eating utensils, breadsticks, the menu, the waiter—anything you can get your hands on.
2 Always smile when you say no.
3 Be formal, not familiar.
4 Avoid long silences, so he won't think you're waiting for his kiss.
5 Yawn repeatedly—tell him you took some cold medicine—and say you simply must go to sleep.
6 At the end of the date, say firmly and politely, "It was really nice to *meet* you. Good-bye!"
7 Arrange for a girlfriend to "accidentally" happen by your table at the restaurant and ask her to join you. Have prearranged code words that let her know if she has to rescue you: Goldfish, for instance, means great date, get lost; shark means help! At that moment, your friend will realize that she lost the keys to her apartment and invite herself to spend the night at your place.

Phonetiquette Between Dates Two and Three

After the second date, phone conversations get considerably more cuddly. The most playful place to chat is the tub. Even if you've just finished getting dressed, it's back in the bubbles with you, babe. What do you mean your phone wire doesn't reach as far as the tub? Buy a new phone wire, sweet doll! The bath call is an essential part of a Love Goddess's reality. Telepurr "Hellllllooooooo" into his ear and ask him,

"Do you mind if I take you into the tub? I was just *slipping* in when I got the urge to call you." Make lots of sound effects, like turning the water on and off and splashing playfully amid the bubbles. No matter what you happen to look like at this moment (mud mask, shower cap, and callous cream), you'll have conjured up an image of you, the Hollywood glamour-puss. Take him through the entire bath with you, right down to the toweling off and the slow application (starting from your neck and working down to your toes) of your favorite scented body cream.

♥ THE THIRD DATE

This is the most difficult date of all. You're practically overcome with lust by now yourself. You get that glorious, dangerous, special, aching-girl feeling every time you think of him—which is all the time. You want him so badly, you find yourself living in a beautiful blur, a sweet cloud of glowing warmth that completely overcomes you. Your GG has stirred something in you, and you find that even though he's the real object of your desire, you begin to wildly project your fantasies onto anything even remotely male that crosses your path.

You need to be in control but you feel that nothing less than a chastity belt will keep you from giving in completely. He's been patient and good, but tonight, you know, he'll pull out all the stops and go into his naughty boy's bag of tricks. It is, after all, time for him to try to enforce the TDR, which is as basic to being a man as a wet dream or the *morgen harte* (look it up in a German phrasebook, *Schatzi*, or just think *hard*).

Wouldn't it be perfection if you could carry me in your purse, like your own personal Fairy Godbabe, to help you keep up your willpower—or what I call Brillpower—through the fateful, thrilling third date? Well, here's the next best thing. A script for a dream date—just him, you, and me:

ANDREW MACPHERSON

Scene I: Your dressing table

YOU: Whatever shall I do? He's so gorgeous, so smooth, so sexy! I know I won't be able to resist! O, help me, Fairy Godbabe!

FG: Relax, Novice Goddess. You've been primping for five and a half hours . . . he'll be putty in your pretty little hands! Just don't forget your chastity belt!

(*Ding! Dong!*)

YOU AND FG (*in unison*): He's here!

YOU: What should I say?

FG: Say nothing. Open the door and smolder till he kisses you!

(*Kiss! Kiss! Kiiiiiiiiiissssss . . .*)

FG: H-m-m, with a date that starts this feverishly, maybe you'd better hand over the key to your chastity belt. No, not to *him*, to *me*.

HIM (*astonished*): Darling! You look even more beautiful than you did when we met. Could it only have been forty-eight hours ago?

YOU: Thank you, my love. It's all for you.

(*Then you step away to give* him *a head-to-toe glance.*)

YOU: M-m-m-m-m. Nice. Very, very nice!

HIM: I'm glad I hired a car and driver for the night. I won't be able to concentrate on anything but you.

✷

Scene II: The limo.

(*You slide into his arms and kiss endlessly.*)

HIM: Uh-oh, I forgot . . . something important at home. It will only take a minute.

YOU: Gasp!

FG (*encouragingly*): Don't worry! You can fondle it! I mean, handle it!

✷

Scene III: His place

HIM (*walking into kitchen*): I'll fix us a cocktail.

FG: Great. Now's your chance to check out his closet. You can't judge a book by its cover but you *can* judge a man by his closet!

YOU: Ooh! Lots of cotton and cashmere, natural fibers . . .

FG: Good sign. But what's this? Shoe trees? Sandals? *Oy*, shoe trees in sandals!

YOU: Uh-oh! He's coming!

FG: Not yet, he's not! Quick, wiggle on over to the window. Your figure stands out beautifully in silhouette.

HIM (*hands you a glass*): To you!

FG: Stand with your back to him and toast him, raising your glass with your left hand while looking over your shoulder. Look down, all the way down, and then up to his fabulous face.

YOU (*following FG's routine to the letter*): To you, and your gorgeous shoulders, handsome!

(*You sip, put glasses on the coffee table. He takes you in his arms and the smooching resumes.*)

FG: Whisper something to distract him!

YOU: I'm melting. No! I mean, my ice is melting!

(*He goes to freshen the drinks.*)

FG: You're catching on, babe! Go put on the last three songs of the sexiest-sounding record in his collection.

(*He comes back in. You dance . . . close . . . closer . . . closest. He maneuvers you onto the sofa.*)

YOU (*after some long kisses*): Oh, I love this! I love . . . this . . . music!

FG: The songs are over, doll!

YOU: Would you mind turning the record over?

FG: Good move!

YOU: O, Fairy Godbabe! With kisses like that, I'm willing to forgive him the sandals *and* the shoe trees!

FG: Never forgive sandals! But I thought I spied a pair of motorcycle boots in the back of the closet, so it looks like maybe there's hope.

YOU: I don't think I can hold back much longer!

FG: Think about it like fencing: Seduce and withdraw; seduce and withdraw; seduce, seduce, touche!

(*He comes back, sits down beside you.*)

FG: (*fierce whisper*): Kiss him into the upholstery! Let him *feel* what you're thinking at the moment your lips meet! That's a goddess! Now, plant your hands on his chest. Pull him toward you. Look him in the mouth, then the eyes. Push him away! Give him that devil-kitten smile. He's disheveled but mesmerized. (*You take an ice cube from your glass between two fingers and lick at it delicately.*)

YOU: I'm starving!

FG: You're also on your own!

YOU: No!

HIM: You're *not* starving?

FG: Don't fret: You'll be safe in the restaurant, and I'll catch up with you later. Right now, I have to contemplate the closet dilemma. Let's see: Maybe the maid put the shoe trees in the sandals; maybe the sandals were an ugly gift from his little sister—does he have any little sisters???

✷

Scene IV: Your doorstep

FG: How was dinner?

YOU (*dreamily*): Dinner?

FG: That good, hmm?

HIM: Darling, we had dinner. But I wouldn't mind coming up for . . . dessert. (*He kisses you*). Something sweet . . .

YOU: Ooh, I'd love to. I really would. But I've completely lost interest in chocolates since we met. I'm afraid I haven't a thing to tempt you with. (*You kiss him back.*)

FG: Okay, here's where he says he'll settle for just a cup of coffee.

HIM: Oh, you're more sweetness than any man should be allowed. How about just a cup of coffee?

YOU: Amazing!

HIM (*running his hands gently through your hairdo, more insistently along your neck*): Does that mean yes?

YOU: Oh, how I wish it did. But it doesn't . . . darling.

FG: Kiss him quick! Hard!

HIM (*groaning*): You don't know what you're doing to me!

YOU (*purring*): Don't I?

HIM: I really would like a cup of coffee.

YOU: Of course, darling. Wait right here and I'll bring it down for you.

FG: Seal that promise with a kiss!

HIM: What?

YOU: Of course. I couldn't deny you . . . a simple cup of coffee. I've got some yummy (*kiss*) French (*kiss*) roast.

HIM: Mmm. That's okay. I guess if I can live without you, I can live without the coffee.

(*After some more seriously fervent embracing, you disentangle and begin to float up the stairs. You pause at the top step, turn to find him still staring at you, and blow him a final good night kiss.*)

FG: Wait! Check it out: He's handing you his tie!

HIM: If you won't sleep with me tonight, sleep with this and think of me.

FG: Mmmm. He's got style! Kiss the tie, press it to your breasts, go in alone, and shut the door. Good night!

✆ Phonetiquette Between Dates Three and Four

In the best of all possible worlds, your GG will rush to the nearest phone booth and you'll be hearing his ring as you walk into your apartment. If that doesn't happen, give him a day. Two if you can bear it. But realize that he may be one very confused twelve-year-old at this point. He may not know what kind of game you're playing. He may not think you're playing fair or, worse, that you don't want him sexually. After all, he's endured all your "no-no-nos" and failed to enforce the TDR, so you may have to call him to let him know that you want him as much as he wants you.

You have two options. If you're a chicken, call when you know he won't be home and leave the most lasciviously promising message you can think of. But a gutsy Sex Goddess makes more romantic use of her Princess phone. Call him late at night, just before going to sleep. Tell him it's like being in bed together. Sort of. Murmur sweetly to him for a while, but when you say goodnight, don't let him hang up. Say: "If I wake up in the middle of the night, I'll reach for the receiver and be able to hear you, breathing deeply in your sleep." Whisper quietly until you both drift off together. Note: Long-distance lovers may wish to install a WATS line.

♥ THE FOURTH DATE

This is it. The moment we've all been waiting for. You—Margot, Miriam, Anita, Gina, Janis, Nina, Gulli, Sandy, Kelly, and all you other pussycats—are going to get what you deserve. You've been very, very good. Now you're going to be even better. In fact, you'll be your best.

You will pack your tiniest evening purse with all the necessities for an overnight date (see box ahead).

You will take the full six hours to dress for this climactic (and will it ever be!) fourth date, and it should take almost that long to *undress*

How to Detox from a Man

It's one of the nastier facts of life: Some men really do abide by the TDR. Despite all your promises of pleasure to come, there is always the possibility that the GG is nothing but a RR (real rat) and will not call for a fourth date. In most cases, you should be able to let this slip over your shoulders as easily as a silk chemise. But what if he got to you—really got to you—and you're pining for him desperately?

Here's a method taught to me by a very bewitching witch for detoxing from a man. It can be used at any time during a relationship when you want to be rid of him once and for all:

1 Take one white rose and leave it on the windowsill so it soaks in the moonlight overnight.

2 The next day, drop the rose into your morning bath. Hold the rose under the water and pluck the petals off one by one while saying his name. You may want to add an unaffectionate term for him as you chant. For instance: "Rick, *icch*; Rick, *icch*" or "Bob, slob; Bob, slob".

3 While soaking in the tub, gather up the petals and pour them over your head.

4 Put them in a chic paper shopping bag and walk to the nearest crossroads (anywhere there's an X, as in *ex*, get it?).

5 Take the petals out of the chic paper shopping bag and throw them over your left shoulder, one by one, while repeating his name and the same unaffectionate term. Success! You have thrown away that person's influence. Now, go buy yourself a dozen red roses and a pint of chocolate-chip ice cream. Detox is complete. Tomorrow, go boy scouting!

STOCKING THE OVERNIGHT DATE PURSE

1. Sunglasses—le must for le morning after.
2. Foundation—sample size or pour a little into a Ziploc bag.
3. Lipstick—to double as blush.
4. Eye pencil.
5. Compact.
6. Perfume—sample-size bottle. Remember: same guy, same perfume, always! Secretly spill some on his pillows so the next evening he'll be sleeping with your fragrance.
7. One stocking (in case one runs, or to be mistakenly left behind drenched in perfume).
8. Money—more than you need.
9. Condoms: two to four, you can always hope, h-m-m-m-m-m . . . .
10. The not-to-be-forgotten key to your chastity belt.

for it. You've been so perfectly patient, you don't want it to be over in the blink of an eye, do you?

But you will start having sex the moment he calls for you tonight. Everything you do will be a form of foreplay. The way you get into the car—slowly, sensuously, bringing in one silk-stockinged leg and then the other. The way you scoot over to sit next to and nearly touch him (sexier than touching him—the air between you will be electric!).

He is your Dark Knight, your Super Hero, your hunky, handsome, Ultimate Heartthrob. You are his Sex Goddess, his Supreme Seductress, his Love Angel, the one babe different and better than all the rest. It will come to him in a rush: You are the brilliant light at the end of the long, seemingly endless tunnel of looking-for-love. You are each other's every wish come true.

What's the perfect setting for this night of passion? Pick a place that corresponds as closely as possible to your wildest fantasy. For instance, if you dream about a dastardly, dazzling swashbuckling pirate who kidnaps you, find yourselves some sort of boat.

All evening long, don't raise your voice above a whisper. That way he'll hang onto every syllable that slips from your so-sexy lips. Now is not the time to talk about anything but the two of you. You may even be so bold as to preview, verbally, what will happen later, in the flesh. In other words, tell him what you intend to do to him! See how much he (and you) can take.

The one thing you should avoid discussing is your romantic pasts. There are only two people on earth this evening: you and he. You don't want him to read you a list of his former girlfriends, how they got together, why they broke up, blah, blah, blah. While he wants you to be the best lover he ever had, the sex diva—and you will be!—he *does not* want to know how you got that way. So keep your history a mystery.

However, this only applies to romantic history, not sexual—you have to at some point have the "Safe Sex Chat." Nobody likes this part. My advice is to do it completely away from a sexual setting and just dive in. Deep breath, big smile, maybe a foreign accent to add some levity to this serious and uncomfortable conversation: "So, I am not an intravenous drug user, nor have I ever slept with one, and, in addition, I am not a homosexual male. What about you?" Naturally, he will say the same. And you know that you cannot trick the truth out of anyone in regard to this highly publicized and important stich. *So use condom sense!*

You're in your place or his place or some heavenly hotel suite. You stand, poised to be pounced, in the dimly lit room, the darkness airbrushing you into beautiful perfection. The scent of your perfume wafts through the air, luring him. It feels as if the entire planet is tingling in anticipation. He comes toward you. You open your arms to him. The date is over. Let the love affair begin!

♥ SEDUCTION BEYOND SEDUCTION: HOW TO HEAT UP A HOT THANG

Now that you're into date five . . . and beyond:

—Read sexy books out loud to him in bed; best is early on a relaxed Sunday afternoon, curtains drawn.

—In a public situation—lecture, wedding ceremony, pre-business meeting—discreetly slip your G-string into his pocket.

—Wear costumes! The moment he picks you up for a date, put your hand on his forehead and tell him it feels like he has a temperature. Casually mention throughout the night that he looks flushed, feverish, etc. When you go home together, disappear and make a quick change into your nurse's outfit—hig heels, white stockings, and don't forget that red cross. Wait for him to come and find you. When he does, tell him Nurse ("Your Name Here") has come to take his temperature . . . but you won't need a thermometer to feel the heat rise!

—Keep that single-girl sex energy, that seduction power, going strong throughout the relationship. When you need to get into that state of mind, give yourself some distance from him. Literally—hang with the babes and flirt like crazy with other GGs. Watch how easy it is to excite a new man—and bring that excitement home to your Number One.

—Change environments often. Borrow a friend's apartment or any hotel, from the lap of luxury to hotel hell. Give him the key ahead of time and tell him to be there at nine o'clock. At five to nine, leave a trail on the floor for him to follow: dress first, shoes, stockings (one at a time), garter belt, bra, then G-string. Leave your jewelry on! As soon as you hear the key in the lock, slip into a candle-lit bubble bath for two.

—Make him an audio sex cassette. Aaaah, my loves, this is an extremely important addition to limitless lust. He'll take the sex cassette with him wherever you can't be. Warning: Remember—just like those nudie Polaroids of yesteryear that may be in the bottom of your ex's drawer somewhere, you must have no regrets. You must feel free to trust your

GG enough to make this torrid tape for him. And as a precautionary measure, never use *your* name, only *his*.

Okay, let me give you a technical approach to the purely emotional act of tape love.

1 Call a few phone sex lines to know what *not* to do.
2 Make a mental outline following these steps: a) gentle introduction; b) slow buildup; c) peak; d) soft resolution.
3 Pick background music, nothing kitsch or cliché; no seventies disco; nothing with another woman's breathy moans; no Top 40 tunes that might inspire him to sing along instead of listening to you. Music must be the distant background of this cassette. Choose something that you love and that makes you feel uninhibited, fully sex-heated, and that lasts as long as you do (an obvious music change or edit makes it sound rehearsed).
4 Get comfortable. Pick a room where no noise will intrude, not even the sound of the phone. Lock all the doors . . . or not . . . whichever makes you feel more wanton. Make sure temperature is right.
5 Begin the tape with a simple hello, using his name. Then tell him in detail about a sex dream or fantasy starring the two of you.
6 Pick something to wear that makes you feel *SEX*! Take it off or put it on while taping. Tell him what you're doing while you're doing it.
7 Once you start taping, your mental outline will come to fruition naturally. Now, here's the hardest part, my darlings, but nevertheless, the most important: You must be sincere and true. In other words, he must hear the real experience when he listens to this intimate time with you. No faking! (Intensifying your reaction isn't faking.)

Once the cassette is made, you have to get it to your GG. The next day, listen to it, and if you decide then to send it to him, there's no turning back. Write a love note to accompany the tape:

My Sweet Darling,

This cassette is *just for you!* Make sure to be absolutely alone when pushing it in.

Dreaming of you . . .

XXXXXXXX

P.S. My player is waiting for your response.

Now, to get the cassette to him: Fed-Ex to his house (not his office!), leave it under his pillow, sneak it into his Walkman, pack it into his suitcase, or slip it into his inside jacket pocket.

Okay, now you babes have my repertoire of dating, romancing, and seducing tips. Employ then as they suit you—and your GG(s). Should a love reaction come about—through fate, fire, and a little gentle manipulation—*brava!* Enjoy it, relax into it. The fantasy you've spun will meld with the reality you are—without you (or him) even realizing it, they will be one and the same. Keep your humor with your GG, and nurture a little "machisma" so the *ultima* fantasy babe in you is waiting and ready when you want her.

CHAPTER 3

Diet: An Inspiration

Weight is a cultural condition. A media condition. The desire to lose/gain weight or become any particular shape is based on a collective image, somebody else's idea of the woman of the moment. Today's concept of the ideal bod is different from that of the past and probably won't resemble the accepted fab figure of the future. Because there's no such thing as a timeless, ultimate proportion, there's no such thing as a timeless, ultimate diet.

I'm a perfect example of this phenomenon. I'm 5′9″ and my measurements, right now, are 39-23-39. I get bigger. I get smaller. A couple of years ago, at my most grand, I was 43-29-42. So you see, size isn't the issue. What you do with it is.

I've busted all the stereotypes. I model on the fashion runways of Paris. The mannequin manufacturer Adel Rootstein, which every decade picks one woman to represent the shape of that time, selected me as Body of the Nineties (in the sixties, they picked Twiggy). The life-size, anatomically correct window mannequin that Rootstein made of me proves that big things are happening. But that almost-living doll stands as a monument to the freedom of choice that all women have. You have the right to be the body type that you are at any particular moment. The key, I believe, is that you have to completely embody the ideal of that body in all respects. What that means, babe, is truly believing that your bod is the best bod.

KEVIN DAVIES COURTESY OF ADEL ROOTSTEIN

Which one is the real D.B.?

This is easy to do when your figure conforms to what's currently considered the media body of the moment. It's more difficult when your shape is in any way different. You have to feel that your uniqueness makes you superior. Not that you should force your body type on somebody else. In other words, don't tell some skinny sister: "Here, you really need a box of bon-bons, babe." Simply feel secure in the knowledge that what you've got is special and deserving of adoration. Only if you have the strength of this conviction will you have the Great Guys of the world eating out of your hand.

During my 43-29-42 phase, I was out on a date with a rock star, who, like a lot of rock stars, was 5′7″ and about 140 pounds. All evening he kept telling me: "Dianne, you're such a body of work! Why aren't more

girls shaped like you?! You're a girl from another world! Look at you: You're a planet unto yourself. You're your own planet—Planet Brill!" An original, articulate compliment, to be sure, but he wouldn't have said it if he hadn't picked up the vibe that I was confident and convinced that my body was the ultimate body.

I'm not talking about too much of a good thing, the extra poundage that makes you unhappy or unhealthy. I'm not an evangelist to the poor sufferers with serious weight problems. What I'm saying is you have about ten to fifteen pounds of absolute leeway. And you can be at your most gorgeous and sexy at either end of the spectrum.

So ignore what your family, friends, and the glamourexic "bulimic moderns" are pushing on you. I suggest trying on a few different shapes, a few different weights, to find the you of the moment. Be a bit bigger, a bit curvier. Or let yourself go to the lighter side. Sometimes you want to take up more space, or hold on to more. Other times you want to float and feel airy, *in* it but not *of* it.

Whatever weight you choose to be, it takes commitment, especially if you want to change the shape you're in right now. Bigger or smaller, you've got to diet your way to the dimensions you desire. But that four letter word D-I-E-T doesn't have to be H-E-L-L.

HERBERT SCHULZ

Then: The bigger me. Feel gorgeous and the GGs will find you. See!

BIGGER

If you want to be bigger, you've got to eat, dress, walk, talk, and stand the part. You've got be big and be proud. These are some words to forget, to completely eliminate from your vocabulary: Fat. Overweight. Pleasingly plump. Full-figured. "Healthy" (the way some people say it, with a sneer). Replace them with the reality: Ample. Round. Female. Womanly. Hour-glass figure. Voluptuous. Curvaceous. Supersensuous. Generous. Warm. Repeat these words to yourself; make them your motto and your mantra for your body of the moment.

The Get-Big Diet

If you're going to get bigger, you've got to do it right. It's got to be quality weight that you gain. I'm not talking junk-food frenzy, I'm talking about indulging in the finest. This can be easy! Eat what you want when you want it. Do not say no to any culinary pleasure. Eat until you don't want any more. Decide what decadent delicacy you'd love right now with no limitations and go and get it. Get two!

During get-big times, I never exercise intentionally. I do, however, hang out with sportsmen—they always eat well. Eat sexy foods that nourish the skin, hair, and nails. Sweet whipped cream is perfect. Imperative: Eat only the *best* chocolates, because in my experience they're more emotionally satisfying than junk chocolate and their pure ingredients won't sabotage the complexion as easily.

Cook expansive gourmet meals for your GG. Make enough for an army. He will adore you for it, and God knows, after dinner, with you, the chocolates, and all that whipped cream, this hunk will *need* the strength of that army.

Clothes for the Bigger You

The bigger you are, the more formally you must be dressed. Big, you have the ability to be luxurious and elegant but you lose the freedom of being too casual. Think of yourself as a marble sculpture, a Venus. Have you ever seen a skinny Venus? You have to be regal.

When you're at the grand end of the scale, you're always on, always obvious. You can't get away with the slightest bit of sloppiness in your attire. Think fastidious. Think neat.

Perfectly manicured nails, glamorous makeup, clean, well-coiffed hair, no wear and tear on shoes. The disheveled look is not for you, babe.

Clothes for the bigger you must fit correctly. That means not too tight, of course, but also, not baggy, blousy, or anything that looks as if you're trying to hide. No sacks, no Morrocan tents or collossal caftans. Best on big women: well-tailored suits, impeccably cut dresses. Show the *right* flesh: as much cleavage as you can comfortably expose. Low necklines are a must. Also, three-quarter-length sleeves or strapless tops. Skirts can be long or short but must be fitted all the way; its crucial to have a long line from hip to knee.

Wear luxurious fabrics. Opt for solids, not prints. I hate prints! They distract from shape, and shape is the true objective here. Dark colors keep lines clean and shapes distinct. Wear black, deep, dark red, midnight blue, forest green. You can wear white, but only something extremely fitted.

No rings—they pudge up the hands. No clunky necklaces—they shorten the neck. Wear bracelets and earrings, only—the bigger the better. Shoes must be high of heel, low of vamp, and never too tight. Lingerie must be beautiful and sexy *always*. No department store "fat people's" underwear ever! Stockings, the finest quality, and always black. Guys love nearly naked voluptuousness; they give everything they've got when you inspire then with your being. With your soft skin luminous in satin and garters, envelop him. Be generous. He wants all of you. Now give that boy what he deserves!

Being Big in Public

You must have the relaxed confidence to make this adventurous experiment work. With the new, bigger you, you'll find that you're the first to be noticed when walking into a room. Stand tall. Posture proud. To accentuate your curves, never stand with your weight equally balanced; keep one leg slightly ahead of the other and shift weight to your back leg—the forward knee should be bent in a bit. Posture is so important: Imagine that someone has tied a string between your breasts at the center of your bra and is pulling up! Shoulders go back, boobs go out, butt perks up, head goes high. Make your gestures smooth and grand. Walk long and strong, happy and directed, to go with your elevated stature.

Your voice has to fit your size. No screeching or squeaking, nothing too gentle. But you don't want to be a bullhorn, either—overpoweringly dominant. Balance is key. Visualize your voice as you speak: see it as round and warm as you are.

When you're in a restaurant, everyone will be watching. Even if they're not, tell yourself that they are, so your table manners will be a work of art. Order whatever you want as long as you don't order more than your date does. Never talk about food—that's the main obsession of people who are unhappy with their size, fat or thin; it's also boring. If he asks if you're enjoying your fettucine Alfredo with extra cheese, say "Yes, thank you," and move on to how heartbreakingly handsome he is.

Don't be afraid to show that you love food: A hearty appetite for eating signals a healthy hunger in other areas that your date will surely appreciate. Licking whipped cream from a long-handled spoon should be done carefully, as if licking honey off a thorn. Eat slowly, as if you're doing a striptease. Savor every bite. Offer him a taste of your dish. Allow him to spoon-feed you a bit of his. Always order dessert, even if you only sample it. If you feel a twinge of guilt, remember that ice cream gets rid of garlic breath.

Soon you'll find that other women are saying to you: "I wish I had the confidence to look like you." Smile, give her a hug, and compliment her on something about her that you really like, whatever she has that's big on her: breasts, hips, bottom, this curve or that curve.

The Heavyweight Date and Where to Find Him

The guy you go out with when you're big should be big too. Smaller men will definitely be attracted to you, and you should feel free to treat them to some of your Amazon appeal. But you'll be most comfortable with a man of your own stature—a heavyweight date—both publicly and privately. Go for the muscle men, huge male icons, and invite them to lie in your lap of luxury. Now's the time and shape for you to indulge fantasies of construction workers, cowboys, uniformed gentlemen, athletes, lifeguards, and bodyguards.

Where to find your heavyweight date? Sporting events are a great hunting ground, also sporting goods stores. Big and Tall Men shops, too: The clothes may be a polyester nightmare, but the shoppers, stripped down, are of natural fiber. Motorcycle shops are good, as are garages—it's always time for a tune-up! Stables are stocked with studs. Health clubs are full of pumped-up bodies. But remember, only hang out, don't work out!

You and your big guy will look as if you belong together—a god and goddess direct from Mount Olympus out for a night of fun. Everything fits. Sexually, a heavyweight is your match. You don't feel that you could crush him with a caress. You can be as wild as you want without fear of breakage.

And speaking of sex, seduction becomes a bigger, more dramatic affair when you're big. Sex Goddesses are generally larger than life. You can get away with more extremes in behavior. For instance, grabbing him to your breasts, growling throatily, throwing *him* up against a wall—all these antics might seem silly done by a smaller seducer, but they're natural for the big one.

SMALLER

Now try another weight, a new you of the moment. Think of your weight and size as you do your wardrobe and makeup options—things you can change at will.

You'll know when the time is right. When it happens to me, it's usually triggered by a new man. For some reason, this lightweight loverboy makes all the big and tall men melt into my history. I decide that if an explosive guy like this exists, there are other lightweights out there, heroes all, hundreds of new men. There is heat under 6′2″ and 180 pounds, and at least 50 percent more men. Instead of walking into a room and only looking up at the heads above the crowd, you can also look eye level or sea level. Ooh, men! Men! I love men! All of them.

Horizontally, however, lightweights are not as dense as meatier men. Holding them, they seem to float. So, sex being the great motivator that it is, I believe you have to get lighter to lustfully pursue a lightweight date.

Slenderness allows you more latitude in your dress and posture. You can sport anything from that messy, just-laid look to pulled-together chic. That's the obvious benefit of being the smaller you. Getting there, however, is more of a challenge. Respond to the challenge!

Let's be honest. Dieting to lose weight is rarely as much fun as dieting to gain. We've all played the same games with food. Like ordering the French onion soup and promising yourself that you'll only drink the broth. You sip the broth . . . and then maybe taste a few onions . . . until they're all gone. Then the softened crouton bread starts calling to you. Next thing you know, you're scraping the dried, cold cheese from the

MIKAEL JANSSON

Now: The smaller me. I'm small and I'm proud.

outside of the bowl and glowering at the waiter who asks: "May I take this, Madame?"

Dieting while traveling is also tough, between the standard fattening room service fare—club sandwiches available twenty-four hours a day—to the chocolates on your pillow. The only benenfit to traveling when you're trying to lose weight is if you have some severe jet lag—I don't know how or why, but you can eat whatever you want and not gain an ounce for one day after crossing an international time zone.

So, doll, to get smaller successfully, you have to get into the right frame of mind. Dieting is a state of mind as much as a state of body. Forget all the negative associations linked to losing weight. This will be a lot simpler to do once you've been happy, sexy, and irresistible at a greater weight.

The Starving Ovation

Here's a diet that will get you smaller faster than any other. It works for me. It's a quick-fix, short-term diet to get you into a new dateshape in a few days (i.e., it's Monday and you've got a date with a lightweight on Friday night). No, your family doctor will probably not approve, so you must not go on this diet for more than a few days. The Starving Ovation is low in calories but high in sensuality, because it acknowledges—and satisfies—the important physical experience that eating is. The Starving Ovation allows you the three main tastes you crave: salty, sweet, and spicy.

Purchase the following:

- Instant miso soup with seaweed.
- Mustards by the millions—Dijon, Grey Poupon, Coleman's Hot English, Honey Cup (ask your grocer; also distributed by Dean & Deluca

in NYC or write to Stone Country Specialties, P.O. Box 133, P.S. "S", Toronto, Canada, M5M 4L6).

- Carrots—the big ones that make clerks in the grocery store nudge each other while you pick them out.
- Celery.
- Progresso Minestrone Soup—cook it and immediately strain out the solids, to be thrown away with a defiant "Blech!" keeping only the broth.
- Orange juice—fresh squeezed if possible.
- Grapefruit juice—fresh squeezed if possible.
- Apple cider.
- Celery juice.
- Flat mineral water—le must, babes, at least two liters daily.
- Fizzy mineral water.
- Hot sauce.
- Coffee—black is best; use soy milk if you must.
- Slim tea—a natural Oriental appetite suppressant available at health food stores.
- Celestial Seasonings tea . . . any or all of them.
- Vitamins—a multivitamin, Vitamin C, B-complex.
- Protein supplement—taken daily with orange juice.
- Other supplements—calcium-magnesium, iron, kelp, Spirulina.

THE REGIME:

Wake up: Miso soup, a grand, big bowl. Vitamins, coffee with soy milk, apple cider, room-temperature flat mineral water.

Later: Raw celery with Grey Poupon mustard as dip. Orange juice or grapefruit juice cut with fizzy mineral water.

Later still: A carrot, eaten whole, no cute little strips. Dip into Honey

Cup mustard. This is my favorite hot and sweet combo. Large glass of carrot juice. Large cup of slim tea.
Much later: Miso soup, large bowl. Don't feel compelled to finish it. Orange juice or grapefruit juice with mineral water.
Last supper: Progresso Minestrone prepared as described above and given a dash of hot sauce. Celery and carrots with Coleman's Hot English Mustard. Celery juice. Mineral water. Large cup of slim tea.
Dessert: Delicious thoughts about GGs. Cut out pictures of them every day, keep them under your pillow, on the fridge, in the cookie jar. Oh baby, oh baby—lightweights! Just look at them. Ahhh! Now go to sleep . . . and dream.

The Smaller-Still Diet

This is phase two of my diet plan—between the Starving Ovation and the Smaller-Still diets, I lost forty pounds. Breakfast is the main meal, dinner the lightest. As a vegetarian, I strongly recommend eating only tofu for protein on this diet—it's healthier and I believe you'll lose more weight. However, if you must, substitute two ounces of lean fish or chicken for every four ounces tofu.

Purchase the following:

- Tofu—age, raw, cooked, tamaried, or baked.
- Fresh fruit—apples, pink grapefruit, oranges, lemons, papaya, canteloupe, honeydew, strawberries, peaches, nectarines (the biggest ones you can find).
- Fresh or frozen vegetables—romaine, spinach, mushrooms, red cabbage, snow peas, asparagus, all roots, no corn, potatoes, or other starchy stuff.
- High-fiber crackers.
- Flat mineral water.
- Coffee—basic black, or with a drop of milk . . . no cappucino!
- Tea—herbal or otherwise.

- Tamari sauce.
- Assorted mustards.
- Dressings—diet salad dressing or olive oil and sweet vinegar.
- Diet soda—cut with water, to flatten carbonation (too many bubbles makes burping or worse!)
- Diet mints—but don't overdo them; sorbitol orgies will make you gaseous . . . beware.
- Orange juice—only for a fast real-sugar fix.

THE REGIME:

Breakfast: Five high-fiber crackers, one large apple, four ounces tofu sautéed with a drop of tamari sauce, coffee, or tea.
Post-breakfast: Two glasses mineral water.
Pre-lunch: Vegetable snack, like mushrooms dipped in mustard, with two glasses mineral water.
Lunch: Four ounces of baked tofu, spinach with diet dressing or a little olive oil, and sweet rice vinegar, five high-fiber crackers, quarter honeydew, or half canteloupe.
Post-lunch: A few diet mints, two glasses mineral water.
Afternoon snack: Peach or nectarine, coffee or tea.
Pre-dinner: Two glasses mineral water.
Dinner: Four ounces of tofu cooked with salad dressing, assorted vegetables, steamed in water, mustard, and sweet rice vinegar (use as a sauce), mixed salad, coffee, or tea.
Late night munching: Hot fresh-squeezed lemonade, as much as you want, with diet sweetener.

So, you say this diet seems fine except for one thing: You can't stand tofu. Substitute the following milk shake for any kind of tofu requirement—believe me, you won't recognize the main ingredient once you mix it up.

RECIPE FOR MOUSSETIQUE DU JOUR

Ingredients:

- 8 oz. plain tofu (firm)
- 6 big strawberries (or any other fruit)
- juice of one lemon
- 1½ tsps. vanilla extract
- 4 packs artificial sweetener
- 5 tsps. water
- Additional spices (to alter flavor): cinammon, Chinese Five Spice, pumpkin spice, chocolate extract

Directions:

Cut up firm tofu, put in blender. Add other stuff. Blend (Rrrnn). Taste it. Is it grainy or lumpy? (Yecch.) Blend more—(Rrrrnn)—until smooth like mousse. Taste it. Too much of this? Add more of that. It's simple. Now, Sugarpuff, indulge in a luscious, creamy luxury that is still on your diet. Check that out. Eat with a small spoon (to make it last longer). You're welcome.

The Staying-Small Power Plan

Eat this way and you'll maintain your smaller size.

Purchase the following:

- Guar gum (natural fiber in capsule form, available at health food stores).
- Mineral water.
- Measuring tape.
- Scale.
- Notebook.

DIANNES DIETRIX

- Stick photos of cute guys on the fridge.
- Every other day, rent an exercise tape. (Do not buy it because you'll be more inclined to use it if you have a time limit.)
- Write your goal weight on your wrist. Like a crib note, a private wish-tattoo, look at it throughout the day.
- Use extra-strength breath spray as a snack!
- Keep your hands busy: brush your teeth, do your nails.
- Be wary of phone feasts: calories consumed while on the phone *do* count.
- Get guys to chase you . . . terrific exercise.

THE REGIME:

- Take four natural-fiber guar gum capsules with two glasses of mineral water half an hour before meals.
- Eat whatever you want but leave half on your plate (you'll find this easy; you'll be satisfied because the guar gum expands in your stomach).
- If you start to doubt that your proportions aren't what you'd like them to be, measure up.
- Get on the scale and write all the numbers (weight and measurements)

down in your notebook; don't do this every day, only when you feel yourself getting bigger.

- If indeed you are getting bigger, start writing down everything that goes into your mouth into your notebook—no cheating. This is a helpful device—if you have to put it on paper, you'll put less in your mouth.

The Lightweight Date and Where to Find Him

Just because you've shifted into a smaller you, don't think for a second you should avoid great big GGs of the strapping linebacker variety. However, the smaller you may yen for a lightweight date. Maybe you see him as a candy substitute, a sort of reward for all that diet discipline; or you want to see what it feels like to sit in the back of a tiny Italian sportscar with someone; or maybe you just feel wispier and airier by a lightweight's side. Whatever the reason, indulge in a lightweight should the desire strike.

- Backstage at rock concerts.
- Museums, bookstores, lectures: Intellectuals are often lightweights.
- Political organizations: The bigger they get in politics, the bigger they get in girth, but anything pre-senator is a lightweight date.
- Casting calls: The camera adds ten pounds.
- Art supply stores: A lot of artists are starving . . . even if they don't have to be.
- Macrobiotic restaurants.

So, my darlings, if you choose bigger or smaller for your next body of the moment, the most important thing to know is: You have to be absolutely, through-and-through committed with complete, unshakable devotion to your current statistics! Until, of course . . . you change your mind.

ANNIE FLANDERS TREATING THE CAMERA TO HER CONTOURS

DELLIAH DOUGH: SHELLS IN PLACE

ACTRESS JENNY LUMET FLAWLESSLY FEMALE

NELL CAMPBELL IN A CLEAVAGE DELIGHT

FABULOUS FREDERIQUE: I BOW TO PERFECTION

GRACE JONES IN LOW-CUT SPLENDOR

NINA HAGEN WITH WILD PAIR & FRANCK

BETWEEN-SHOOT BOOB ADJUSTMENT

ON THE SET IN COSTUME: TERESA GILMORE

BENJI IN MY DESIGN: THE BRILL BRA

PHOTO: ADRIAN BUCKMASTER / SAVEL INC.

FIBERGLASS BOOBAMANIA

CHAPTER 4

Boobs

When I was a little girl, I used to sneak peeks at my father's *Playboy* magazines to pick out the breasts I wanted when I grew up. "Please, God! Give me big boobs!" I'd pray, hands clasped to my nonexistent bosom. Since I knew God helped those who helped themselves, I passed into puberty with training bras, fiberfill bras, and stuffed bras at least two sizes too big.

Then, after seventeen years of being "Dianne Brillboard," it happened. They happened! And they kept right on happening. At thirty-nine indomitable inches, my prayers had been answered.

Lots of women think that men are breast-obsessed (and indeed they are!). But we put a lot of thought into our boobs, too. A woman's body image is largely dependent on how she feels about her upper torso—how she feels about her bod has a lot to do with how she feels about her boobs.

FAB BOOBS FOR EVERY BODY

I've been blessed with large breasts, and let me tell you, they were worth the wait. Because having big boobs (or BBs, for short) gave me an extra uplift of confidence, a top-of-the-world attitude. They work perfectly for *me*. However, BBs are not best on every body. All boob sizes have their fans and supporters.

I'm very up front when it comes to big breasts. For my silhouette, they're grand—the bigger the better. Yet not every woman feels that way about hers. Many babes have confided in me about the burden of having gygo-bosoms. Most often, they were early bloomers who all of a sudden felt ostracized. They couldn't play touch football with the neighborhood boys anymore! The guys who were their buddies started making the wrong kind of passes at them, and laughing about their fronts behind their backs. These young girls were being treated *sexually* for something that was strictly *physical*—and there's a *big* difference between sexual and physical development. Translation: These babes got their boobs too soon . . . and they haven't gotten over the trauma. The timing was wrong . . . but the timing is *right* now. Once a woman's sexuality has caught up with her anatomy, she can truly understand her advantages.

Personally, I've never considered big boobs a burden. If men are attracted to my bosom, that's okay with me; and if they can't get beyond my boobs, that's *their* problem. As my friend writer and editor Stephen Saban, once said, "Dianne Brill is two of the best things in life!" He also quipped: "Dianne Brill—abreast of the times!" I am the mascot, the extreme example of bosom freedom. I stand up for breast pride, a celebration of spillage (my coinage for cleavage). I represent the beauty that is bosom—yours, mine, and ours.

You have great boobs. Believe me, you do. They may not seem so to you, but like all other aspects of the Goddess Complex, boobs are a matter of attitude more than inches or consistency. Size, for instance, is such a subjective thing. Think about it: Your boobs are bigger now than they were when you were on the brink of adolescence, right?

Firmness is also subjective. In the hands of your man, your breasts are sublime! He loves the way you feel when he's holding you, even more maybe than if you were made of saline or silicone because whatever shape they're in they belong to you, and you and *yours* is what he wants.

Remember, it's not what you've got; it's what you think you've got (and what they think you've got) that counts! If you *think* you've got fab boobs, you do. Thrust them out! Flaunt them forward!

Maybe you feel your boobs are "too wide apart," "too pointy," "too round," "too droopy," "too perfect" . . . oh, you babes: Shut up! DIANNE BRILL IS HERE TO TELL YOU THAT *YOUR BOOBS ARE THE BEST IN THE WORLD!* Feel it. Feel *them*. Your proud tits. Believe. You believe, we believe, he believes. I said it, and that should be proof enough. But here are some snippets of interviews between myself and some more very experienced boob experts (men)!

Beauty and the Bust

GG #1: Rock star. Inviting, very sexy and intense. Single.

GG: Why I like small-breasted babes (SBBs)? They have to be attached to the right person. Just because she has a certain type of breast—medium or large, for instance—doesn't mean I'm not going to be excited by her.

DB: Yes, right, of course. But you did say SBBs were your favorite. Why? Forget you're talking to a BBB, just answer, handsome!

GG: Well, ummmm . . . SBBs are elegant. You know, like Louise Brooks. And I think in sex, the nipples are more in my focus, well-displayed. And there are some aspects of the naughty little girl thing . . . but wait a minute, I don't want a little girl, I want a woman in bed with me! *Look, I love SBBs, and I know they are the best in the world.*

DB: Okay, so you want more proof: Read on . . .

GG #2: Promoter, heartbreakingly elegant, luxuriously handsome, has a low voice and a diplomatic air. Single.

DB: You have a strong reputation for being a BBB-worshiper. Explain, please.
GG (*Laughter*): It's likely I love the BBB because, more than others, she is, to me anyway, feminine. All the way female. I've always considered myself overly masculine. I need an overly feminine woman to keep me feeling, well . . . you could say balanced. When I'm naked with her, one of the most incredible times has to be just staring at this vision of soft femininity knowing my face can just get buried in her breasts at any moment. This is a delight I hope I will never have to be without. *I love BBBs and I know they are the best in the world!*

DB: What a guy! But keep reading, there's more . . .

GG #3: Actor. Huge puppy-dog eyes. Quiet, thin, muscular. Drives a fast car. Stares directly into your eyes when he talks to you. Single.

DB: So you say you like every kind of breast. Cool. But come on, you dreamboat, forget the sell . . . name your *real* favorite.
GG: No! Truly! I can tell you that in my experience, every shape and size breast has its particular advantage or intrigue . . . sexually, anyway. In most aspects of life, I'm a very possessive man, and women with large breasts get a lot more attention in public. This makes me nuts! In making love I find that if I pay a lot of attention to a woman's breasts,

any kind of breasts, the more I spend on this concentrated area, the more I touch her, the easier and more relaxed she becomes with me. Maybe because I let her know by showing her how *I* feel about her breasts, she's more confident in a sensual way. Most men are like me, I think. You know what I'm saying. But I do find the more self-assured *she* is about her breasts, the more I'm attracted to them. *I love BBBs, SBBs, all BBs, and I know they are the best in the world!*

DB: Well, check that out! Didn't I tell you? *YOUR BOOBS ARE THE BEST BOOBS IN THE WORLD!* Whatever your size, you are A-mazing, B-eautiful, C-ductive, or D-lightful!

Changing Your Boobs

You still have the freedom to change your boobs if you want to. Smaller or bigger. Bigger or smaller. The obvious option: plastic surgery, which has improved many a babe's profile and perspective by increasing or decreasing her size. And surgery is so popular and available these days. Even radio stations have had contests that give away implants to the lucky caller.

Surgery however, is not for everyone. You do, after all, have to go under the knife, which can be frightening. Besides, when you have plastic surgery and you're laid up for two weeks, there are possible complications and nobody gives you that bedside sympathy—and the flowers and chocolates that go with it; instead you get: "You wanna be more beautiful? You gotta pay!"

Fortunately, there are other ways to make your present endowments even greater. For one, there's the power of a truly great bra wardrobe, which I'll unfold for you in uncensored detail come Chapter Five, the Sex Goddesses' guide to lingerie. But most important—I said it before and I'll say it again—is the way you feel about your breasts. If you don't wanna think big, you gotta think proud!

Aren't we all
A-mazing, B-eautiful,
C-ductive, and D-lightful?

The *Real* Pencil Test

All right, doll, admit it—you've tried it. The test that runs regularly in magazines that tells you whether or not your breasts are all they should be. You're supposed to judge shape, size, and firmness by placing a pencil under your breast. If the pencil falls, you get an "A" for firmness. But the truth is you'd have to be smaller than an A cup, a little girl, or a male to pass this test. Inaccurate and impossible, all this test does is convince you that whatever you have is wrong.

But face the facts, babes: They're wrong. *Very* wrong.

Any babe with more courageous contours should take *my* pencil test. This will establish the truth about the beauty of your breasts. In French, there are about ten thousand words for cleavage. My favorite is *le balcon.* It means "the balcony." *Your* balcony. With the bra pushing up and pushing in, straps extra taut to realize your maximum spillage potential . . . *voila! Le balcon* is formed. And it's the kind of balcony that your many Romeos will be desperate to scale.

Now for the test. Begin by putting on your sexiest, *balcon*-accentuating brassiere. Now take that pencil and slide it between your breasts. Does it stay? Yesssss? You passed the test! *Magnifique!*

Boob Envy

Some guys suffer from a condition known as boob envy. It's the flip side of women's penis envy. These guys believe that women have power and other advantages based on their breasts. It all comes down to this: You've got something they don't. Namely boobs. And this makes them jealous.

Simply the vision or the outline of a breast is sexy. Big boobs are often considered sexiest because they are overt symbols of the female. Nipples showing through a blouse are sexy. Unless you try very hard (and why?) to disguise them, your breasts are on display. People notice them. And that's sexy. A man's foremost symbol of sexuality—his penis—is never as obviously visible as a woman's breasts (unfortunately!). Therefore, the envy is understandable: A woman can't help but show her symbols of "sexuality," while a man must keep his tucked inside his trousers.

Another reason. Breasts are always sexy, whether or not the nipples are erect. The male organ, isolated in its relaxed position, is generally *not* considered as arousing. So men may be bothered by the fact that their symbols of sexuality have to be in top form to be considered hot stuff.

So now you understand what's behind boob envy, and you're no doubt wondering how to deal with it. Basically, you have to build his self-esteem about what he has got, not what he hasn't got. Specifically:

1 Recognize the maleness he keeps between his thighs as erotic in *all* stages of development, from half past six to twelve o'clock high!
2 Notice and appreciate his obvious assets—shoulders, nipples, butt, thighs . . . whatever you like. Concentrate on them to the point of fetishism!
3 Avoid staring directly at a guy's crotch during normal conversation. This is not only rude, it brings up every insecurity his mind has to offer.

Boobs in the Boudoir

Umm, in case you haven't noticed, boys love boobs. They exist solely for a sample of your ample bosom. They love to look at your breasts, dream about them, touch them, etc. (yes, even those plagued by boob envy). So to think of your boobs as anything less than twin idols made for worship would be sort of blasphemous, wouldn't it? You must always present your breasts in the best possible way, and this is most important in bed.

Take a large hand-held mirror to bed with you and examine how your naked breasts look from all sides. Some views will be tantalizing—remember those positions and get into them to tease and please. Other angles, however, will not exactly accent your assets. Lying down on your back, for example, can cause some breasts to go east and west. Avoid this when posing for him—always keep your arms close to your body when you're stretched out, pressing in a bit to make the most of your mounds.

If you like the way your boobs look in a beautiful bra, keep the bra halfway on during lovemaking—leave it clasped but lift your breasts out of the cups.

One more thing! All breasts look their best when aroused. So feel confident when you're in bed with him—if you feel good, you're lookin' good!

The Public Boobs

"Booballure" is logical: Eyes are naturally drawn to a person's outstanding feature, and boobs are double outstanding because there are two of them. So play them up when you go out.

For your "time for fun" times, dress in a way that displays what you've got:

1. Buy your sweaters in the children's department, or get them a size smaller. (When clothes fit snugly, you're constantly aware of them, and awareness is always an advantage.)
2. Go for plunging V-necks, deep scoop necks.
3. Wear your low-back dresses backwards.
4. Don't buy your blouses too tight, as buttons on the verge of bursting look tacky. But do unbutton them as far as you dare, giving the world just a peek at your peaks.
5. Whatever you're wearing underneath, reveal a taunting glimpse of lingerie, an especially nice contrast if the outfit is fairly conservative.
6. Position jewelry strategically.
7. Don't forget that invisible but essential final touch! Perfume the valley between your breasts *generously!*

8 SBBs can go braless and blouseless under a low-cut one-button jacket; when wearing a blouse without a bra, button just one button at the waist and tuck the blouse in tightly at the waistband of your skirt.

Wherever you're going, whatever size you are, lead with your breasts. Keep your posture erect, shoulders back, head poised to further highlight the dynamics of your dimensions. Never slouch in an attempt to hide your boobs; nor should you ever cross your arms over them. Instead, cross your arms *under* them to lift, lift, lift!

Of course, in social situations, you might find yourself in the middle of the "battle of the boobs." That's when you dress for a party in an outfit you thought was almost indecently risque when you left the house but looks like a nun's habit compared to all those other girls in backwards black dresses! Don't let this become a cleavage competition—it's simply not good babely behavior to drop an ice cube down the front of another doll's dress. Better to revel in the nonsexual but definitely sensual experience of being breast-to-breast with your fellow Sex Goddesses.

You may meet a man who cannot tear his eyes away from your spillage. This isn't necessarily bad, depending on the source. If he's a real bore, if he's rude—you know, this guy is an ogling ogre—shoot this clod a blank, look over his shoulder for someone else—someone who can appreciate you in total—and take a walk.

Believe Me About Boobs

In 1982, Annie Flanders, genius of spotting trends and trendsetters, put me on the cover of her mag *Details*. She caught on quickly to the fact that I was starting something big. She wrote, and I quote, with complete self-indulgence (after all, this is *my* book): "Dianne Brill wears her tits so proudly and so blatantly that it's become catchy. Dianne has come along and made us proud of what we've got. We've liberated ourselves enough now to be able to look like women again and hold our own as it were. Dianne is our leader. Although I expect that in a year or so, some famous designer will come out with a line emphasizing breasts, (They all did, and do now, have you noticed? No brag, just fact) and be lauded for bringing them back. But for this one, Dianne Brill should definitely be credited." Aaah! Now I really feel like the Queen Bee . . . or should I say the Queen BBB!

OFF SET: ME & MY TRAILER

L.A. LIMO-SHOPPING LUXURY!

BLACK G-STRING ON VACATION IN FLORENCE

RED BRA & LITTLE BLACK BOOK

BLAZE STARR & TERESA GILMORE

ANTONIA LANGSDORF (M.C. LOLA) SHOWS OFF HER NEW WHITE PURCHASE

L.A. FREDERICK'S OF HOLLYWOOD

QUICK! WHERE'S THE SHOPPING CART?

COFFEE: THE PAUSE THAT REFRESHES

IN PARIS, STOCKING HEAVEN: SHARED WITH A LOCAL BABE

CHAPTER 5

Lingerie

Frederick N. Mellinger, or as we know him, Mr. Frederick of Frederick's of Hollywood, has a sign posted in the small museum inside his glamarama L.A. store. The sign, nestled amongst bras worn by everyone from Madonna to Milton Berle (don't ask!), promises: You may come in looking like a Chevy but you'll leave us a Cadillac.

Good imagery, if you check out the chassis of, say, a 1963 Cadillac: hot and shiny. Fins pointing up and out. Headlights round and smooth, perfectly positioned. Proud, lavish bucket seats. Windshield wipers batting like eyelashes worthy of the most exquisite Southern Belle Babe. Lingerie does indeed do what Mr. Frederick says: It transforms you into whatever sort of Sex Goddess you feel like being at any moment. Harem Honey. Titillating Tigress. Angel Baby or *Diablesse*. All the fab facets of your personality.

Lingerie has special sexual power in all cultures and all countries. The English have a fabulous eccentric kinkiness that goes to extremes,

Doesn't Fastnacht look like fun?

with housewives in vinyl and rubber babydolls. Italians want ultramodern up-to-the-second fashion, fashion, fashion—for instance, if leather trim outerwear is of the moment, the Italians will be wearing leather trim underwear to match. The French are obsessed with old-name quality chic—the Hermès "Kelly bag" of lingerie look.

And then, there are the Germans! They celebrate the freedom lingerie brings in a most unusual holiday! It's like the ultimate Sadie Hawkins Day! In Munich, they call it *Fasching;* on the Bodensee it's *Fastnacht;* in Dusseldorf, they call it *Karneval;* but in Berlin, they choose to ignore this custom. On this special occasion, women get dressed in costumes—basically, lingerie, with masks to hide their identities. They roam the streets with scissors, clipping men's ties from their necks and tying the bits of ties together, proudly adding them to their costumes. Later in the evening, when the holiday reaches fever pitch, Fraugangs form. These packs pick an unlikely seducee—you know, like those boys on the street who tell you something *really* original like "ooh, mamma, I'd love to have a piece of that, yuck, yuck, yuck"—and then they strip him of his clothes and leave him dumbfounded in the *strasse.* Speak to your travel agent—the textbook name for this holiday is *Altweiberfastnacht,* and it takes place in February.

You reinforce your Goddess Complex with every sexy shred of lingerie. Your lingerie wardrobe is your private U-world, your underworld of enticement. Each gorgeous undergarment fuels your unique "thang" and helps project your aura.

LINGERIE: IT MAKES THE LOOK

No matter what you wear for the public eye, it's the U-world that makes it happen. The look—that amazing black moiré bustier cocktail-shaker dress—just won't work if your underfashions aren't doing the right thing.

Or how 'bout when you're in one of those in-between times. You know, you're not this shape or that shape, you're not committed to being bigger and curvier or smaller and finer. The proportions are off and you're on the wrong side of the right weight. What to do? Pull it in? Push it up and out? Lingerie will improve those proportions. It will glorify and reglorify your body, celebrating your assets (all your sets, for that matter!) and playing down any parts you're not as interested in showing.

To make the most of your totally sexy self, let's fuse illusion into reality. There's no such thing as a perfect body. You know this! But, with the U-World, you can add (and/or subtract) inches anywhere. You have control! Cinch your waist to nothingness. Pump up your boobs. Tame your hips. There are bras that best display your dangerous curves, panties that make every bottom beautiful, garter belts that show off legs so firm and smooth in stockings worn at the correct placement for *your* height and size. Come on, dolls, do the most for your fab, feminine self. Ready? Okay! We'll take it from the top and work our way down.

Shopping for Your U-World Wardrobe

Where to find the best in lingerie? Catalogues are great, because you can order as much lingerie as you like and return or exchange as necessary. Plus, you try everything on in the privacy of your own home. That means no annoying saleslady barging in while you're arranging your breasts. It also means you can do a little boudoir fashion show for your GG, and let his reactions guide your selections.

There are plenty of lingerie catalogues around, but as far as I'm concerned, Frederick's of Hollywood is absolutely unparalleled. It carries an incredible assortment of curve-making, bust-boosting, flesh-flaunting beauties from the basic, everyday underwire bras to those naughty little numbers with the cut-out crotches. So get yourself a subscription!

Of course, you can also shop for bras in department stores and lingerie boutiques. If you're in the market for long-line or pointy-cup bras, check those old-fashioned lingerie stores. Think only the over-80-years-old set shops there? Think again!

STEVEN KLEIN

Aah, the bra!

TLC for Lingerie

Discover the wonders of lingerie and you'll never think of it as mere underwear again. That means you'd better treat it right! Revere your brassiere! Be good to your garter belts! Pamper your panties! Never toss lingerie into the laundry bag the way you would a dishtowel. Hand wash your loving cups and dainty drawers with scented, colorless soap and let them air dry. Keep them in a dresser stocked with heavenly sachet.

AAAH, THE BRA!

The bra is the best invention known to Babekind. The right bra will create and enhance spillage so that you appear fuller, rounder, and ooh-la-la-larger. Right now, the most popular bra promotes the melon-shaped breast, but there are other contours to explore. The snow-cone! The ski-jump! The global collide! To push up and point out your future, pick the kind of bra that does the most for your bosom. Here's a rundown of bras and what they do for your boobs, plus specific selections from the catalogues—Victoria's Secret and Frederick's of Hollywood, foremost, and some others.

1 Underwire bras are the basis of good support. You don't have to wear a harness, but the bra must be well constructed. All your everyday bras should be underwire; they promote that firm, pert, slightly pointed shape that looks best under basic blouses, sweaters, T-shirts, etc. A little bit of metal is not like wearing a suit of armor—if the bra fits right, the wire won't bite.

   For a fierce figure (cup sizes A through C) wear a pretty underwire bra with a demi-low front; be sure it lifts well and separates. If you wear a D-cup or larger (all the way up the alphabet to FF) buy a bra with a strong racer back—a bit of a sexy saddle (make sure it fits or the curse of flub-back will get you!).

2 Push-up bras, riding high, push up and push in for every babe (yes, all of you who've moaned that they do nothing for you). The secret is to buy them one size *larger* around and one size *smaller* in the cup. For instance, if you're a 34-B, you'd buy a 36-A. The bra will fit higher in the back, but accept it if you want non-compromising cleavage. Also, be sure to tighten the shoulder straps about two inches shorter than you do for any other style bra. Cup your breasts, arrange them up—they are pillowed into place, forcing all the flesh in the vicinity into spectacular spillage. Push-up bras are necessary under anything low-cut.

   There are different styles of push-up bras. Get a multifunction or convertible one that goes from regular to halter or criss-cross. Expose fabulous femme flesh in the lowest cut push-up you can find—the cups look like crescents that barely cover your nipples. For good global collide with limited overspill, get a push-up that has extra reinforcement on the sides of the bra, to push in as much as up. Push-up bras that are semi high cut make globes stay put and show just a taste of your top shelf; great for low necklines.

3 Padded bras, your top secrets for a ravishing, fuller round shape. Crucial: Fasten 'em tightly so the padding won't be apparent in any position. These bras are best with tight lycra tops and dresses. (If you're thinking about implant surgery, test out several different sizes by wearing padded bras). Padded bras can add a little or a lot (as much as two cup sizes) . . . and Frederick's, undisputably, makes the best.

4 Pointed or spiral-stitch cups give you that ultra-pointed, exaggerated, sweater-girl shape. Long-line versions act as waist cinchers, and when your middle looks smaller, your bust automatically becomes bigger and more beguiling.

5 Nipple-exposing bras create an incredible optical illusion—they have structure to lift your breasts, but the cut-out points display the nipple. It's a fetish bra because you are wearing this for sex, pure and simple! Men love 'em! The best of these bras lend some support while baring the nipples. If you want to show your nipples through your clothing, these are the bras!

6 No-bras make for nipple exposure in the extreme—they basically expose the entire boob: simply a wire to push the breast up with an inch or so of bra.

7 Strapless bras are not my particular favorite—you're better off with a long-line corset for a smooth look—but for daytime, they're less restricting and they do the job. The best styles offer support, push-up, and pads.

Invest in your chest, and it will become your greatest treasure. That doesn't mean buying only expensive bras—most often they are the least sexy, so why bother? Of course, there are exceptions. Brassiere couturiers who custom-make the bras know boobs like no one else—bosoms are their business and they are dedicated to their craft. This luxury is available in most large cities, usually dedicated to oversize—like 46 triple F—women. But they will make any size in any fabric at your request (or your insistence). The best brassiere couturier I know is London-based Rigby & Peller on 2 Hans Road, SW3, though they concoct some very sexy (silk, satin, you name it) contraptions, they are the official bra-makers of the Royal Family.

Cheap bras are always fun and usually sexy (we all know when cheap means it doesn't cost very much or when cheap is *cheap*), so buy a bunch in all shapes, sizes, colors, and fabrics. Just be conscientious and retire a bra as soon as it begins to show signs of wear. Never, ever cradle your cleavage in worn cups or pooped pads. The elastic of the straps must snap like new. The clasp must be easy to fasten—and unfasten.

A CRASH COURSE IN CORSETS

The full push-up corset is a staple must for your U-World wardrobe. It's a posture perfector in the classic full size (ends at the waist) or in three-quarter length (ends at the hip). For every day? Of course not! But, at night, in a bustier dress, that firm, high, round decolleté . . . hmmmmmm. Spillage pumped up, creating you in a gorgeous vision of all the best things that the beautiful balcony has to offer.

A full-corset classic takes some of the fleshy sides of your chest, pushing in and up, and combines it with your breasts for an incredible display. This is why when you see most photos of women pre-1970, they look like dream goddesses in their bustier dresses, while too many women look sloppy and unattractive in such a daring cut now. Well, put these same modern babes in the correct undergarment and they will achieve dream goddess status.

The design and engineering of such corsets is genius. True, they're not the most comfortable contraptions—you'll probably say ouch the first time you lay eyes on one—especially when you're sitting down a lot (then they can really bite). Wear a corset occasionally, let's say for a special party. In time, you'll get used to it, and the results are worth it. Your waist and midriff are slimmed into nothingness while your hips stay rounded and smooth. You should wear a corset with the attachable garter belt tabs and stockings: It holds up the stockings, and everything is kept in its place.

One corset I like is by Lady Marlene. Ask for the classic #986, with ribbon trim (have your dry cleaner, seamstress, a friend, or you—take it in at the waist to build in even more shaping for a whistle-slim look). Lee's Marti Gras Boutique in New York City has great, colorful, exotic corsets. Trashy Lingerie in Los Angeles makes the deepest low-cut V-front corset, custom-ordered in everything from black moiré rayon to red velvet with gold braid and pearl trim. Of course, this is extravagant. I suggest you start with Trashy's basic black, ultra low cut, three-quarter corset.

Aha! But what about what not to do in this contraption? Don't bend forward too much or too often or you risk the possibility of a BOOB EXPLOSION! Kaboom! Right out of the corset cups. Instead, do the Bunny Dip:

The Bunny Dip

A move established in the Playboy clubs, beginning in the sixties, to avoid any accidents. Playboy Bunny cocktail waitresses, while carrying drinks and placing them on the table, were discouraged by the management from bending over in their bustier bunny costumes. Don't laugh! *Now* it seems absurd, but some very important women have hopped down the Playboy Bunny waitress trail, from blonde legend Debbie Harry to Gloria Steinem who did an exposé on the club. An interesting experiment in experiencing the worst sexism first hand, you may think, but my impression of these clubs is that because of the extreme rep Bunnies had, by virtue of the job and the costume, they needed to behave in an almost Mormon-cocktail-waitress conservative fashion to compensate.

Not just for putting something down, but also for picking something up; try it, it's like this:

1. Make sure the object or subject is directly in front of you.
2. Shoulders relaxed and neck straight, crouch down slightly.
3. With knees together and pointing slightly to the right of you (for balance and style), crouch down further.
4. Pick up or deliver with the left hand.
5. Slowly, with confidence and poise, rise to your starting position. Maintain a glint of arrogance in your eye, as you have just mastered an act few could ever pull off with such majesty! Every inch of you is positioned exactly where *you* want it.

WAIST NIPPERS: THEY'RE A CINCH

These are must-have members of the corset family. They're not only super-sexy fetish items, they have a practical purpose, too: All my girlfriends and I know that nippers are great for getting into any outfit during those pre-period blow-up times.

An excellent version for the SSBs is the three-quarter-length nipper. It goes from just under the bosom to the hip, and forms two Us under the breasts—as if the bra cups were cut out of a normal corset. Exposing the nipples and boobs with the U framework, it features your bosom with pride. A must-show-off garment. Buy them a size smaller (they generally come small, medium, large) for maximum exaggeration of your contours. You can lose inches off your waist while accentuating your bosom, creating that enviable hourglass action. Nothing gets flattened out except your abdomen; everything that should be round is even rounder. Of course, all sizes can benefit from this design. It can be worn with or without a bra. Garter tabs with stockings keep the lower half of the waist cincher from popping up while you're sitting down.

My favorite waist nipper is a black satin number with a ribbon lace-

KEN NAHOUM

Nipper: Cincher sensation.

up front and hook-and-eye back (available in many catalogues, such as Victoria's Secret and Frederick's). This is gorgeous on all of us! Unfortunately, because these items tend to be part of the "fantasy market," they're often made of satin acetate (translation: cheap fabric). They have a short life span, so save for special occasions.

GARTER BELTS AND STOCKINGS

You know what garter belts are, girlies! And you know the problem with them, too: They always wind up on your hips, when they're so much sexier-looking on your waist. The solution: The seamstress (or yourself, in a snap). Simply fold it over and hand-stitch it up so that it fits flatteringly on the waist.

Garter belts' function is purely to hold up your stockings. In other words, they don't provide any support or foundation. However, there's a subtle yet indisputable appeal to them. They keep you dressed while undressed. You feel more than naked, welcoming him into your queendom. In conjunction with stockings, they are classic cross-your-leg flirt tools. Also, because they involve more than plain old pedestrian pantyhose, men feel that you've gone to extra trouble to look sexy for them. And, they make you extra accessible when the time is right now!

When worn during intimate manuevers, stockings and garter belts are your battle gear, your armor, your protection. They provide delectable distance, a bit of mystery between you and your lover. They inspire a sense of abandon, a loss of convention and predictability. Garbed in your garters and stockings, you become a catalyst for creative lovemaking. You're you—yet you're a fantasy figure. And fantasy absolutely belongs in bed! (A word of caution: These getups need to be paced! Sometimes leave them on, sometimes take them off . . . it's your decision.)

Fit and positioning are imperative. There are three basic lengths of stockings. Opera length, my favorite, reach highest on the thigh, a few inches below the bikini line. I like this look because it frames and cups the two round cheeks of your behind beautifully while camouflaging and smoothing out thigh flub. Plus, it lengthens the leg—great for the width of the thigh. Also, when wearing stockings to bed, this length tends to shift the least. The trouble is, opera-length stockings barely exist. Sure, on the Rue St. Denis in Paris, you can find them in a shop called Le

Sexy, which caters exclusively to strippers, transvestites, and *us*. If you can't jet out to Le Sexy, buy a few sizes larger, but make sure the heel isn't woven in, or the heel reinforcement will be somewhere around your calf. Another alternative is to buy stockings with four-way stretch—the weave is not so fine, but you can pull them up to opera length. Never buy stay-ups! They slide and/or cause flub at opera length.

MICHEL COMTE

Mid-thigh length exposes the fleshiest part of your leg . . . and men love to feel the silkiness of your stockings melting into your creamy femme flesh. Texture, dahlings, texture! These are the average-length stockings—easy to find. To ensure against flubbing, give the stockings a good stretch in all directions around the upper thigh area.

Victorian-length stockings reach a few inches above the knee. They make you feel like you're not wearing stockings at all . . . you have total and complete thigh freedom. (Be warned: You'd best be well toned to wear this stocking!) These look great worn with staid outfits like longish skirts, giving your GG a wonderful shock to see how nearly naked and dressed-for-sex you are under your chic-cold-fish projection.

Select stockings according to your whim—but always consider what your GG likes (remember, you're dressing for two!). Cuban heel, seamed stockings in light off-black are classics. The Cuban heel is a reinforcement that makes a diamond shape pointing up your ankle, thinning out the area, and the seam acts to round out the calf. Just think of the seam as a fuse leading up to your dynamite.

Slipping Up Seams

To keep the seam of your stockings from shifting:

1 Make sure that your legs are cleanshaven—no stubble!
2 Apply moisturizer to your legs and leave a bit of lotion still moist on your skin (this will help stockings stick where you want them).
3 Turn the stockings inside out—this is a trick for keeping the seams straight.
4 Put your two thumbs carefully inside the stocking and scrunch the fabric up slowly and evenly with your two forefingers.
5 While seated, bend your knee and point your toe. Slide the stocking over your toe and very carefully ease it over your foot and up your ankle, making sure that the seam is centered on your heel.
6 Continue easing the stocking up to your calf.

7 Hop over to a mirror and check it from behind. If it's not even, pull it down to the ankle again and reposition the heel.

8 Pull all the way up and fasten to your garter belt. Be sure that the garter tabs are exactly centered, front and back. Off-centered tabs can shift your seams.

(Note: Always freeze your stockings before you wear them. I don't know why, but somehow, when they're kept in the freezer overnight, the fabric becomes stronger, giving your stockings longevity. Be sure to let them thaw in the refrigerator.)

A word about pantyhose: They work in practical real-life situations and some fashions demand them. However, don't confuse pantyhose with stockings and garters. Crotchless pantyhose, suspender pantyhose (a built-in, flesh-baring effect), and pantyhose with fake garter embroidery are compromises. Sensible sex gear is a contradiction in terms.

Color is a matter of personal choice and outfit coordination but there's one "color" no woman should wear: suntanned pantyhose. A strong "flesh" color—suntanned or not—is a total mistake. The idea of skin-colored stockings is to smooth and highlight your wheels, not change your family heritage. Imagine: She has Scandinavian arms, Arabic belly, Brazilian bottom, Albanian facial structure, Malaysian chest, and Californian legs . . . maybe this sounds like a modern cover girl, but remember, collar and cuffs must match as far as skin-colored stockings are concerned. Choose extra sheer. (Tip: If you've got a bruise on your leg, just use a little makeup. Blend it in with light, feathery strokes and brush on a little powder.)

G-STRINGS VERSUS PANTIES

Panties are a problem. Just about all contemporary fashion has no respect for panties as a U-world option. Firsthand, from movie sets to Paris runways, I can tell you: G-strings or no strings are the only ways to go. Visible panty line is always apparent, even in jeans. And you know what? Designers don't care—with their cling-fit clothing, they're forcing you out of your panties.

Most of you probably love panties. You've worn them since you were a little girl. You're attached to the style. You think they look flattering. The idea of a G-string is uncomfortable to you . . . and that means you probably never put one on.

Before I launch into why I'm such a staunch supporter of G-strings, let me say that I'm a lingerie liberal—wear what you really feel good in. Tap pants, cotton panties, bikinis, or bloomers. A babe with imagination can make any U-world challenge work. But do this Brill a favor, will you? Come on. Just *try* a G-string?

I had a small part in the movie *Blaze*, about the legendary stripper Blaze Starr. I played a stripper, Delilah Dough (as in dollars), and though I never actually stripped, I did wear the most incredible G-strings with pasties to match. In one scene, I jumped out of a giant clam shell, running from the film's star, Paul Newman, who was, gun in tow, shooting up my stage, mid-performance. Well, between waiting around to do my scenes in full wardrobe—on the set, in my trailer, makeup touch-ups, lunch, checking scripts, dishing with the other actors and actresses, giving interviews, and sitting down (a lot!)—that sequined and seashelled Venus G-string didn't pinch, bite, crunch, crawl, or in any way cramp my style. Why? Because it fit!

G-strings are not twisted torments. Forget those one-size-fits-all micro-strings: Unless you are an extra small size, they will cause an outbreak of ouch. Be sure to buy your correct size, and if the G-string looks really skimpy, it is skimpy, so go a size larger. G-strings not only look better under everything, they're sexier than panties when you buy the right size and style. I'm not talking about a rope. What we've got is a half inch of soft fabric that does not cramp your style. Hey, this type of G-string or thong back was originally designed to give ballerinas total freedom of movement, and babe, if you can plié in it, then it's got to be comfortable.

While the thong back is indispensable, you need a wardrobe of sexier strings . . . for sex! In these cases, comfort doesn't count! Go wild! Like orgasms, the more you have, the more you want. There's no law of diminishing utility in collecting G-strings. Look for adornments and tricks to delight him with, everything from strategically placed zippers to, if you can believe it, even the crotchless G-string.

The Subtle Significance of Color

Lingerie is your mood-spectrum color wheel. The shade of lingerie you wear sets the tone for your lovemaking, and the other stuff you do, too. Different colors invoke certain messages, inspire specific reactions.

For me there are three primary colors: white, black, and red. Other colors may be worn according to your whim. And some colors should not be worn at all!

A wise word about white: It looks innocent but it *will* betray you. After one explosive night, the salt from his sweat, the lining of that tight black skirt, the scented soap the color of tangerine that you use to wash your skimpy white whatever-it-is in, the no-stain deodorant stains—all contribute to the short lifespan of innocence. The off-white, gray tint and/or yellow factor is the result.

Beige, nude, and yellow are forbidden. Banish them from your U-world. Beige looks like old white, so forget it. Nude is functional, but somehow prosthetic looking . . . and if you need another reason, men hate it! And yellow? No way! Don't you dare! It's not that I don't adore yellow. In fact, in junior high to my teacher's dismay, I even composed a monstrous, silly ode about it:

Ode to Yellow: My Favorite Color

All the kids in school like blue or red.
Every rock star and teen idol likes blue or red.
But I say yellow is my favorite color.
And I love the little feller.

No one ever picks yellow for anything good.
They use the color yellow to describe cowardly, scared
Or chicken.
They're mean to yellow.
But not me.
Every time anyone asks me:
"Dianne, what's your favorite color?"
I automatically say "Yellow!"
All the kids bellow, "Yccch, I hate yellow."
But I am sure to let the lonely color know
That it has a friend.
Me.

Yellow, my love, you're still my favorite color. Except when it comes to lingerie. Never, ever!

THE U-WORLD COLOR KEY:

Pick a color and check what it means. Then make it happen, you boudoir bombshell!

White: Innocence. Purity. Trust. Bride.
Black: Sublimely horny. Wanting and willing. Hungry, seducing, commanding. Ready (right now!). Experienced. Strong.
Red: Speedy. Insatiable, accessible, in demand. Beautiful for the skin. Playmate. Cliché-risqué. The other first option along with black or white. When a babe wears red, she *means* it.
Fuchsia: Hot bordello babe. Easy, fast. Almost red.
Pink: Playful. Almost innocence. The naughty-but-nice coquette. In deeper shades, especially with any black trimmings, it means subliminal "female triangle."

Gray: Chic-cold-fish.
Nude: Practical. Measured self-denial.
Beige: Subtle to the point of boring. Non-threatening.
Fluorescents: Fashionable fun. Not serious. Not sexy . . . except under black light, then *incredible*!
Blue: Little boy blue is cool but gentle. Naiveté . . . but only pretending. Navy blue is novel—so intriguing but only from time to time—and watch out, it could be chic-cold-fish like grey.
Peach: Always the bridesmaid, never the bride.
Yellow: Remember—don't you dare.

Fabric, Trim, Adornments, Fasteners, Etc.: What They Mean

Don't forget the magic of fabric! Silky, lacy, exotically trimmed lovelies make you feel sexier, so you look sexier when you wear them. Once a lover was smitten by the tiny red rose that rested between my bra cups. "A rose on a rose," he murmured. The very next day, two dozen long-stemmed stunners were delivered to my door, and that evening, when we were together, he took a flower from the vase, touched it to that place on my bra and whispered passionately, "A rose on a rose on a rose." Maybe he was gilding the lily with this compliment on top of compliment, but you see, the right lingerie not only does a lot for you, it can do a lot for your man-thang as well!

U-WORLD FABRIC/TRIM KEY:

Satin: Wet. Slippery. Drapey. Must touch!
Matte Silk: Not nearly as sexy as satin. The old-fashioned-girl look—it has its audience. Some silks feel dry, like antiperspirant, to the touch (avoid them). Must be ironed. Loses dye quickly.
Cotton: Best in G-string or V-backs. Safe. Fresh. Clean. Sportif.
Velvet: Lush. Elegant. Borderline bordello, but at its best.

Fishnet: He'll take the bait. Total "She's wearing these for me!" lingerie.
Chiffon: You can see but not really touch through it. Temptation! Hot in colors. In white or black, from bride to merry widow.
Maribou: Soft. Fluffy. Pettable. Cuddlepuff.
Ribbons: On the sides, to tie and untie—never yourself: Give him one end and say "please pull."
Flowers: See my "rose on a rose" tale, above.
Buckles: Hard. Intense. A lot of work!
Hearts: Sex-magazine sexy in guys' eyes; but makes us babes feel pretty and sweet.
Velcro: Forget it!
Snaps: At the crotch, necessary practicality.
Zippers: If slowly unzipped, very good. Careful—don't snag!
Buttons: Really sexy, because they take soooooooo long to undo.
Locks: !!!!!!!

Okay! I know! You're probably wondering "Locks? On lingerie? Dianne, doll, are you kidding or what?" Well, let me tell you a little lock story.

I was invited to attend the Emmy Awards in Los Angeles and, billed as "Dianne Brill, the Siren of Style," to do a talk show, speaking about the notorious fashion tastes of the ceremony. "Glamma!" I thought. Of course, I was excited about the trip. I love doing TV, and would do a totally Brill job on the show. But the true "out of breath" feeling of dizzy anticipation came from knowing I would soon be arriving in midnight madness mecca, the pyramid of passion fashion. That's Trashy Lingerie (402 La Cienga Blvd.), Frederick's of Hollywood (6608 Hollywood Blvd.), and Playmates (6438 Hollywood Blvd.).

These three stores are situated to form a pyramid. The extreme point is Trashy Lingerie, the custom-designed to overly custom-designed corset, bra, garter belt, and G-string. Members-only heaven. The base points are Frederick's of Hollywood—you know the famous motto: "Add to the illusion of the natural you"—for staples, le must foundations, and some fluff; and Playmates. In Playmates, the supermarket of fluff for the U-World, there are miles of aisles of pasties, G-strings, bras (some covered in maribou), garter belts in royal velvets (some with Baroque studding), jewel-colored gloves (satiny and elegant), fishnet head-to-toe catsuits . . . everything deserving of your complete indulgence. Price tags tend to be inconsistent, but the idea here is volume purchase—yours, mine, and ours. If ever a lingerie store needed shopping carts, it's Playmates.

Well, I felt this *calling.* You know that feeling: I'm going to look through every one of these racks until I find *IT!* That one ultimate G-string, superior to the others. I made my way undaunted through all those tangled little hangers, stashing a few "maybe"s or "why-not"s along the way. And then, there *IT!* was, hidden in the back of the sales rack. Black and gold chain perfection. Tailored with eyelets, linking the chain delicately through the blinding, shiny gold lock. Then, on *IT!*s hanger, I found two keys. Ah! One for me . . . and one for "him" (good thinking!). My self-imposed chastity belt with two keys!

Anyway, I absolutely *ruled* the Emmys in my jeweled Thierry Mugler derriere-exposing dress, did the TV show, and came back to New York. I tucked away my chastity-belt G-string, knowing someday *the* GG would come whom I would want to unlock me. It happened. *The* GG did come.

It was early in our relationship, when everything was fantasy à la mode. Anything goes—you don't have any limits, any right or wrong . . . only creamy exploration. Well, we were somewhere doing something—dinner, I guess—and all night, all I could feel was the presence of my lock. And all I could think about was that I had to leave for Paris the next day. We talked sadly about my departure—the first time we'd be separated since we met. Finally, we drove back to my place.

He was holding me and petting me—ooh, was I dying for him! One problem: In this rolling around and tussling, I couldn't find the key! He kissed me. He touched me. But I wasn't letting him *really* near me

Here's a full frontal

view of derriere-exposing

Thierry Mugler dress,

but for the Emmys

I flew solo.

without that key. My God! I'd been planning this a long time and I wasn't going to call off the game now. He begged me to give him my G-string and I said, "Yes, my darling . . . when you unlock me with the key." He searched me *everywhere* to find the magic key. Begging and searching, begging and searching. It was fun . . . but, the moment of unlocking had come once I spotted the small key in the carpet. I worked us over there so I could discreetly pick up the key, but then he spied it, too. We both jumped for it. I got it! I kept the key and teased him with it. I said if he told me three beautiful things about me, I would give him the key. He did. I kissed him with the key on my tongue. He slipped it into his mouth and then into his hand. In slow seconds, I was unlocked.

Aha! The flip side of this romantic tale happened the next morning when he insisted on locking me up again. I said, "Er, um, yeah, right . . . but, what about you?" He promised his complete fidelity while I was designing a locked G-string for him in my head. I'd go to that neighborhood seamstress when I came back, I thought, but for now, I'd let him lock me up. After all, there *was* a spare key that only I knew about! After the locking ceremony, he wiggled the key onto his keychain, and, following a sweet, beautiful bye-for-now-my-love kiss at the airport, I blew him more kisses and watched him as he watched me walk toward security. I waved good-bye as he passed out of sight, smiling, holding up his key for me to see.

Through the security arches I went . . . and the machine went crazy, beeping, buzzing, and lighting up. I unloaded my camera. My housekeys. Silver belt buckle. Earrings. It keep buzzing! I was late for my plane, of course, so I thought I'd make a joke to the security guy. "Listen!" I said. "Don't worry about me! We sex bombs don't have to carry weapons . . . we're loaded with artillery naturally!"

Now there's one thing to always remember when dealing with members of the security profession of any class, stature, or rank: *They do not have a sense of humor!* Especially when it comes to buzzword no-nos like

ALVARO

My self-imposed chastity belt:
one key for him and one key for me.

bomb, weapon, artillery. I wound up in a four-hour search of my luggage. Linings of coats. Contents of compacts. High heels of shoes (fifteen pairs of black for the five-day business trip). Even my hairdo was searched. And then two huge women took me into a very small room and, while the luggage search continued, the women scanned my body with one of those hand-held metal detectors. Slowly they scanned. Everything was fine. Until they reached this one area. Yes, of course! My locked G-string!

To avoid even the faintest move toward a strip search, I immediately showed the two security women my locked G-string. They looked at each other. Then they smiled at me like two Cheshires from *Alice in Wonderland*—or maybe like Tweedledum and Tweedledee—and asked me to wait. Within minutes, one returned and said I was free to go; they'd arranged another flight. All eyes were on me as I left the little room. I felt wiped out, embarrassed, but somehow triumphant. They treated me like a dignitary, helping me with my bags, escorting me to the plane. I'll never know what Tweedledee and Tweedledum, the Cheshire sisters, said to their superiors to get me and my lock off the hook. Maybe when it comes to matters of the heart, certain things are naturally understood among women, all women—even security women. Or maybe a G-string with a lock on it is the one thing those of the security profession *do* have a sense of humor about.

ANDREW MACPHERSON

The right shoe.

CHAPTER 6

High Heels

High heels are your pedestals. They transform any set of feet into sex symbols. Wear them and you show that provocatively purring, feline side of your sexuality. Know that your high heels are your pedestals, and pose, pose, pose! Great guys will fall at your feet, yes, where all good men belong from time to time. Oh, please be careful not to trip over the mountains of men strewn in your path. Now, little darlin', strap on the T-straps and *work* your wheels.

This is law: Shoes must always be sexy. Why should they be any other way, when there are high heels, higher heels, highest heels, and those specialty items, the at-home-use-only heels, offering all the options. Sensible shoes? They should have heels no lower than three inches. Barefoot in the sand? Nice. But as soon as you reach the boardwalk, it's on with the mules, babe. Believe it, gorgeous, even your bikini feels different and looks sexier.

The right (and left!) high heels have brought fame and fortune to countless women, from Betty Grable to Eva Peron. Forget diamonds (okay, don't forget them, but keep your priorities straight): High heels are a girl's best friend. Imagine yourself in a pair of HHs. Toes pointed . . . arches peaked . . . the length of your leg pulled taut. Exactly like at the moment of orgasm! *Quelle coincidence!* And the rhythm and tempo of your heel taps—click-click, click-click— is the ultimate erotic lure. No wonder the male of the species can't resist your heel appeal.

I am one of those women who were born to wear high heels. When I first learned to walk, it was on tippy toes, and I've been up on them ever since! My feet are just like Barbie's, ever ready to receive HHs. I mean it, I simply *can't* wear flats. For a scene in the movie *Slaves of New York*, I had to jog through Central Park in a pair of wrestling shoes. Well, anything for my art! Between takes, I'd slip on my orthopedic stilettos so my feet could go back into their natural position. Still, after twenty takes of sprinting back and forth, those wrestling shoes totally ruined my feet and I wound up twisting my ankle. Of course, I was off for a vacation when the shooting wrapped and I had to hobble on cobblestones all over Italy.

To me, high heels are push-up bras for the feet. Every member of the Brill Babe Brigade knows she belongs in HHs. So how 'bout it? Snuff those sneakers, fire those flats, lose those ludicrous loafers and treat your feet to the kind of shoes they deserve, doll!

THE PHYSICS OF HIGH HEELS

A pair of high heels creates an incredible illusion, giving thin legs curves and full legs streamlined elegance. But they do more, ooh, much more. Slip on a pair of high heels and your entire appearance changes dramatically. Your upper body becomes majestically straight, providing you with bust thrust. You're instantly taller—by at least three inches—and that automatically improves your posture, head to toe. Height and stance accentuate voluptuousness, making you look Valkyrian on your twin towers of power, while the highest heels or the at-home-use-only heels suggest a degree of coy vulnerability that appeals to the chivalrous nature in men.

The Right Shoes

Gorgeous gams—we absolutely *all* have them. The key is balancing out your imperfections with the right pair of HHs:

Heavier legs: low vamp and elongated semi-rounded toe balances the width and gives an illusion of length. (Note: Be sure the front of the shoe is substantial; a too-skimpy style makes your feet look too small in comparison to the rest of you.)

Skinnier legs: mules and other open-toed, light and airy shoes show more foot flesh and make legs look in proportion. Note any photo of pin-up queen Jayne Mansfield: mules, always mules.

Bow legs: classic pumps with some sort of ornamentation (a bow, a clip) on the outer side of the shoe, near the arch, to draw attention away from the inside of the leg; over-the-knee pull-on boots (avoid calf-high boots).

Is this a well-balanced babe?

I.N.P.

Knock knees: low vamp, bright colors, pretty ornamentation keep the focus on the feet, not the knees.

Short legs: moderate platform in front with thin (never clunky) heel gives height.

Wide ankles: low vamp, dark colors, matte fabric for slimming.

Narrow ankles: high vamp, ankle-high boots, ankle straps add substance. (Note: Don't fasten ankle straps too tightly.)
Biggish feet: low vamp, semi-rounded or semi-squared toes, no ornamentation, high arch.
Smallish feet: high vamp, semi-pointed toe, heavy texture (snakeskin, brocade, suede).
Less-than-shapely calves: The highest heels going work magic on your calf muscles.

THE PSYCHOLOGY OF HIGH HEELS

High heels can affect your mood and level of self-esteem. Sometimes, when I'm feeling a little blue, I march straight to my closet and try on my favorite heels. It works wonders, lifting me out of the doldrums. And shopping for shoes is one of the best bluesbusters in all of Babedom.

What is this intense emotional response that women have for high heels? I don't know—who am I, Freud? Maybe shoes—lots and lots of them—mean that you've made it, you've arrived. When I first moved to New York City, I lived a romantic but budgeted existence: I only owned two pairs of high-heeled pumps. Both were black suede with five-inch heels, but one had a rounded babydoll toe and the other was a superpointy post-punk Winkle Picker. I was in deep. I was committed to both pairs! Naturally, I wore off the nap of the suede and had to refinish the shoes with matte-black spray paint before going out. The smell of paint permeated my apartment and competed with my perfume.

One afternoon, turning to inspect a pair of broad shoulders in motorcycle boots, I snapped off the heel of my precious babydolls. I was horrified! I rushed to the shoemaker in shock, and he informed me that nothing could be done to save the shoe. Still, I couldn't just throw them away!!!!! I tucked them lovingly into their box with scented pink tissue paper and hoped that somehow my heel would heal itself.

Despite my grief, I planned my outfit for that evening (I was on the guest list, for the first time in my life, at a rooftop nightclub). I decided to wear something gothic-gorgeous: velvet, leather, lace, and chiffon, all perfect foils for my Winkle Pickers. But as Fate would have it, just as I was heading down the stairs, the toe of the left Winkle Picker snagged on a step and the heel was then ripped out at its roots. As the tears welled up in my eyes, I thought to myself "Watch the makeup!" Then, resourceful babe that I am, I went back into the apartment and put on my left rounded-toe babydoll and out I went wearing a mismatched pair.

All evening, I tried to pose with Winkle Picker in front, babydoll behind. And I almost got away with it, too, until Julio, who up until that moment was my trusted friend and sometime fashion consultant, noticed my attire. "Diaaaaaaaane!" he cried, his voice rising over the throbbing beat of Teenage Jesus and the Jerks, "you're wearing two different shoes!" I guess he just wanted to interrupt the conversation I was having with a swashbuckling nightclub dreamdate. There I was, new in town, cool-obsessed, and Julio was jeopardizing my performance! In my eyes the world seemed to stop spinning as the club froze, waiting for my reaction. Time stopped, and then, after a deadly silence, I swiveled on my babydoll, glanced down at Julio's feet, crinkled my nose, and laughed icily. "I got them in London," I cooed. Not a great answer, but with the conviction of my attitude and, as anything from London was paramount cool, I managed to leave him stupefied with my "don't you love them?" Then I continued chatting up my pirate-prince, who, by the way, was from London, too.

That night was a turning point in my life. I swore I'd never go shoeless again! My future would be well heeled. As my shoe collection accumulated, I learned the historical derivation of the expression *well heeled*: In times gone by, high heels were the exclusive garb of the royal and the wealthy. Peasants were strictly prohibited from wearing HHs. In today's enlightened society, HHs are available to everybody, but they still retain that aura of privilege that makes you feel like a queen. High heels impart a sense of strength. Wear them and you're in total control, on top of the world. Heels of the most dizzying heights, however, can make you feel just the opposite—fragile, dainty, and delicate.

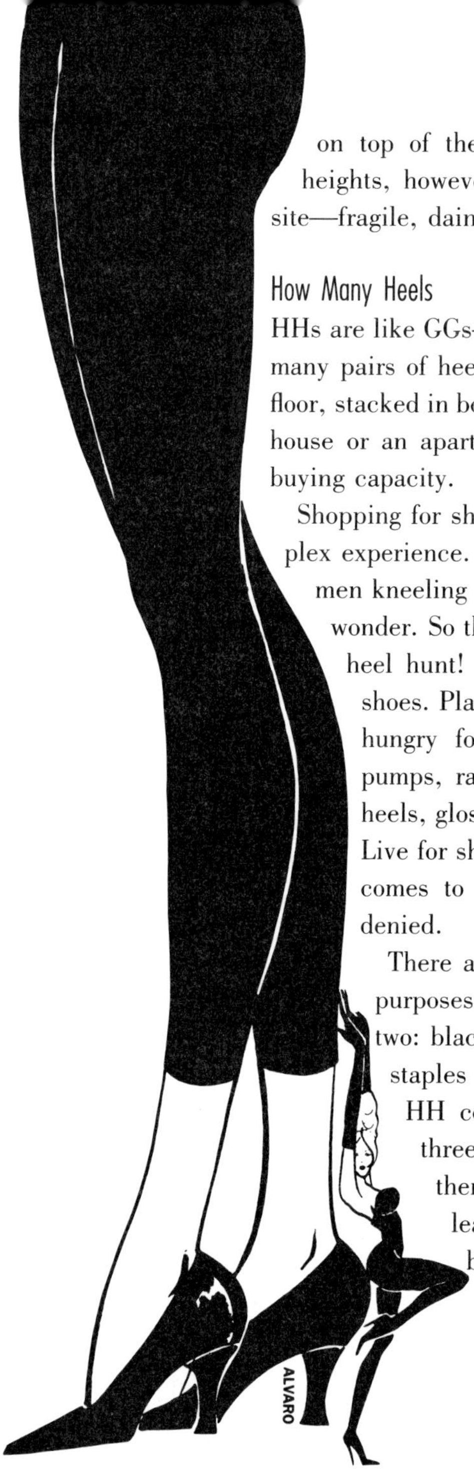

How Many Heels

HHs are like GGs—you can never have enough. Own as many pairs of heels as will fit into your closet—on the floor, stacked in boxes, on shelves. If you have a summer house or an apartment abroad, lucky you! More shoe-buying capacity.

Shopping for shoes is a quintessential Goddess Complex experience. After all, it's the easiest way to have men kneeling before you, worshipping your pieds of wonder. So think of life as one long, glorious high-heel hunt! Every day, at least window-shop for shoes. Plan your budget around shoe buying. Go hungry for a delicious pair of spiked silver pumps, racy red satin booties with transparent heels, glossy green stilettos studded with jewels. Live for shoe sales and really stock up! When it comes to high heels, babe, you shall not be denied.

There are all sorts of HH styles, but for our purposes, to simplify matters, there are only two: black and high-risk. Black shoes are the staples in your stable of heels. Peek into any HH collector's closet and you'll see, say, three hundred pairs of shoes. About 250 of them will be black. Black patent, black leather, black suede, black satin; sling-backs and mules, pumps and platforms, all in black.

ALVARO

When you find a pair of classic black high heels that you absolutely adore, always buy two pairs. You'll know when you've found true shoe-love: You'll feel as if the shoe is an extension of your leg. And that's so important. Shoes must always fit. You cannot diet your way down to a too-tight shoe, and trying to stuff the toes of a loose pair doesn't really work (you cannot properly pad shoes the way you can a bra!). The only exception: suedes—purchase them a half-size smaller or they'll stretch to fit like flip-flops.

All other shoes are high-risk high heels . . . but who said you didn't live dangerously, doll? Indulge in these heels with the same zeal you have for basic black. High-risk high heels are invaluable, irreplaceable, and one of a kind. You know, the four-inch fuchsia suede with lime-green patent-leather trim stilettos that you're saving for just the right outfit (good luck!). Or the party pumps too pretty to wear to a party where your dancing partner may miss a step and smut up those ice-blue silk-satin beauties with the chiffon bows. And what about those nasty hip-high, skin-tight, custom-made sex boots you haven't found a date daring enough to wear for?

Never discard a pair of high-risk high heels for the silly reason that you've never worn them. If they've gone beyond the span

of style, store them away and later be the first to bring them back into fashion.

Always take superb care of your high heels. Your high heels pamper you, so you should pamper them in return. There's nothing shabbier, nothing sadder, than a pair of run-down high heels. Get on a first-name basis with your neighborhood shoemaker. Be sure that shiny surfaces could pass a military inspection and that matte materials are beautifully buffed and free of scuffs.

The Art of Walking in High Heels

It's a fact: A herd of stampeding elephants will do less harm to a marble floor than just one woman in a pair of stilettos. So what? If *you* were a marble floor, what would you rather have all over you, hmmm?

It's not enough to *own* high heels. You've got to be able to walk in them. High heels add a wanton wiggle to your walk. Hips sway hypnotically as you sashay; your bottom becomes rhythmically mobile. Mincing steps create the erotic tempo of your well-orchestrated movements, revealing the Goddess in the walk. A high-heeled saunter is the signature of the sexually confident. High heels are a great guy trap, but you have to get the walk down pat. And that takes practice.

As soon as you buy a shoe—especially a higher or highest heel—hold it by the toe and the base and bend it a couple of times to loosen it up in the center. Never ram or jam your foot into shoes or try to put them on while standing up—the main reason some women say they can't walk in high heels is because they're not wearing them properly. Slipping into HHs should be a slow and sensual experience. Sit down, lift your foot onto your lap, and slide the shoe onto your foot sideways. Twist your foot, opening and closing the space in between your toes, until the shoe feels comfortable. Mmmm, doesn't that feel grand? Do the same for the other foot.

Now stand up and get your balance. Adjust to the new distribution of your weight: Three quarters of it should be on the ball of your foot and one quarter on the heel. Notice how everything, from bosom to bottom, rises up. Consciously push your shoulders back so that you don't tilt forward.

You're ready to move, babe, so put those high-heeled locomotives of love into action. Envision yourself on an imaginary tightrope. At the other end of the tightrope is the most gorgeous hot thang you've ever seen, and he's beckoning to you. Go to him!

Begin with baby steps, putting one foot directly in front of the other. The heel should hit the high wire first, followed by the ball of your foot. Bend your knees ever so slightly. Keep your head held up—lock eyes with that GG. Think about how fab your legs look; be aware of their beauty. Feel them when you walk; concentrate on every sensation. Think only perfect thoughts! When you're walking correctly in high heels, you'll naturally take on a bit of hip-sway and your arms will glide at your sides.

Once you've got the basic walk down, get bolder.

1 Let your strides become longer for a prowly sort of saunter.
2 Try kicking out your feet gently with each broad step, my favorite Paris runway walk, a saucy little stroll.
3 Avoid obvious gyrations, but feel free to subtly exaggerate your strut. Add a bit more bounce, some extra sway.
4 Practice wearing your highest heels with your tightest skirt—the vampiest walk around.
5 When climbing stairs, stay on the balls of your feet and let the heels hang over the steps. Be sure to walk in front of your GG going up stairs and you'll rule from behind.

Before taking your new shoes out for a stroll around town, wear them at home for a while to make them your own. All shoes have a break-in period. You'll walk most sexily in a pair that bears your personal imprint. Because shoes conform to your very own feet, never lend or borrow them. It's okay to try on your boyfriend's motorcycle boots from time to time, but don't let him try on yours.

ANDREW MACPHERSON

When the art of
walking in high heels
has you exhausted,
sit down, relax and
pose, pose, pose.

At-Home-Use-Only Heels

Some shoes should never touch the street. Typically, they have some sort of maribou flourish and a heel higher than the highest. Such shoes are strictly for entertaining *chez vous*. Impractical, you say? Far too frivolous, you scoff? At-home-use-only heels do have some very functional purposes—you'll find that they come in really handy when you're reaching for things on the top shelf of your closet, for instance, or changing light bulbs.

HIGH HEEL EXERCISE

To get your legs high-heel ready, do this exercise every day for a month. Take out the Yellow Pages and stand on it in stockinged feet with your heels over the edge. Get into the stork position by bending the left knee (hold on to the wall for support) and putting all your weight on the right side. Raise yourself up onto the ball of your right foot as high as you can, then lower as low as you can. Repeat twenty-five times, then switch to the left foot.

But the real deal on the at-home-use-only heels is the way they turn an average evening around the old abode into one of endless, intoxicating pleasure! Your man will respond to the sight of the shoes (especially if his perspective is from below) and understand that only you, a woman of complete femininity and grace, could possibly wear them. And don't forget the unique sound of your heels tapping on the floor (every woman taps out a personal signal) will be sweeter than any romantic music. He will want to know these shoes intimately; he'll yearn to fondle them and be fondled *by* them; he'll beg you to let him remove them from your feet and then plead just as insistently to put them back on for you.

Wear your at-home-use-only shoes not only *to* bed but *in* bed. This can really do a number on your satin quilt and sheets, leaving boudoir battle scars all over, but you'll take pride in these torrid treadmarks of love. Here, a few pointers for high-heeled sex fashion:

Foot Flirtations

With your tootsies tucked into a fab pair of high heels, they become flirting tools. Here are some lovely ways to put them to work:

1 Playing Footsie: Go overboard under the table and thrill him at the theater! Nudge his toe with yours or use your toe to explore beneath the hem of his trousers. Rest your foot against his, then remove the pressure, then press against him again; do this in a very spontaneous manner so he's not sure if the contact is intentional or utterly innocent.

2 Cross Action A: When you're seated across the room from a man you want to attract, continually cross and uncross your legs. Do it slowly, sensuously, so that he can imagine the silkiness of your stockings as one leg glides languorously over the other.

3 Cross Action B: Make him tremble in the back of a cab! With both of you facing the same direction, wrap your right leg over his left so it rests between his legs. Swing your calf and point your toe. Quickly and casually, just do it!

4 Seductive Adjustment A: While seated, lean down as if to adjust the base of your shoe, the vamp, or ankle strap. Let your fingers linger on your feet but keep your eyes on the GG who has captured your attention for the moment. This is a position guaranteed to make his heart pound. Between the sight of your cleavage, your legs, your hands, and your high heels, he will be in heaven!

5 Seductive Adjustment B: While standing, lean over from the hips, perking up your derriere and bending one knee naughtily to toy with your strap, heel, stocking seam, etc. When you stand up again, haughtily toss your head, swivel your hips, and give him *that* smile.

6 Devilish Dangling: As you sit with legs crossed high, allow one shoe to slip off somewhat, exposing the tender underside of your foot. Move your leg so that the shoe swings as it dangles from your toe. Practice this move at home until you've mistressed it—you don't want the shoe to plop loudly to the floor and break the spell.

ALVARO

Anatomy of a high heel.

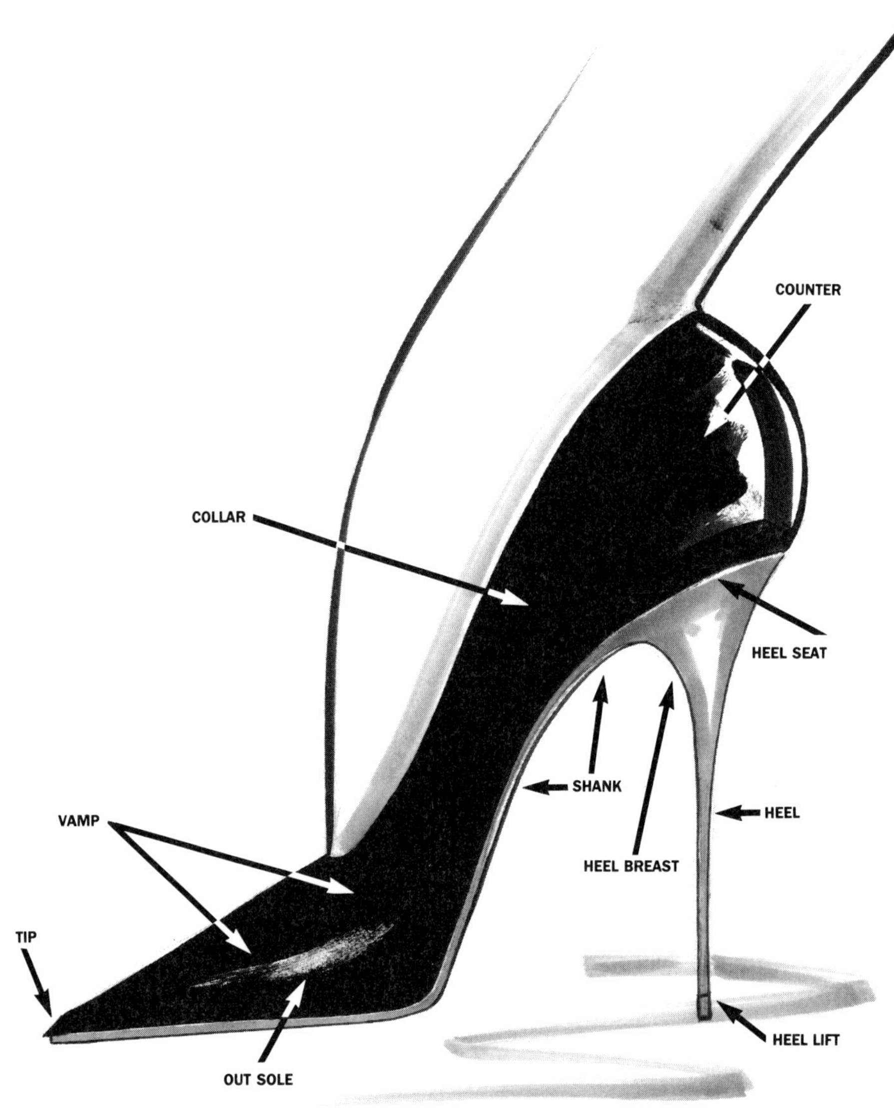

1. When dressing or undressing in your guy's presence, shoes and stockings must always be the first thing you put on and the last thing you take off.
2. If you and your steady GG have had a spat, leave your heels on when you climb into bed and he'll know you want to make up.
3. High-heeled mules make your naked body look its sexiest from all angles. Keep a pair of these sexy slippers at bedside.
4. Thigh-high boots? Never! Boots for the boudoir must reach higher, all the way up to the "firing line." Crotch-high boots feature your bottom best.
5. Open-toed shoes are sheer negligées for the feet! If you're going to wear them, be sure you're impeccably pedicured in a classic shade like red, pink, or simply clear. No butterfly decals or toe-jewels, please!
6. Low-vamped shoes create so-sexy toe cleavage by slightly squeezing the front of the foot.

What are cheap shoes? One night stands.

MARC BAPTISTE

A popular girl on a popular block.

CHAPTER 7

How to Be Queen of the Night Every Night

Nightlife is a dreamy fancy-dress universe where fun is the objective. It's a realm in which you have the freedom to laugh at and with yourself . . . and, natch, those around you. Oh, how the darkness softens the realities that are made for the day, as well as the rules, rights, and rituals of lighttime hours. When the moon comes up, werewolfish transformations go down. The plumber, sans plunger and overalls, becomes a muscled club king. The powerful CEO of a major corporation turns timid yet intrigued by the wild tides of the night. . . .

But nightlife is more than having fun. When you have "multiple-party integration"—meaning, you go to different parties with different types of people, sometimes on the same night—you experience alternative lifestyles and opinions, opening yourself up and stimulating your confidence and your ever-developing character. This makes nightlife an essential forum for learning and trying out new ideas for business, friendship, and love stories. Nightlife is a grand entrance, an introduction into every conceivable arena. Nightlife will open daylife doors. When you become the Queen of the Night you discover that you're more than the life of the party—you're having the party of your life.

Okay. What about this Dianne Brill thing—how did I become New York's "Queen of the Night"? And what, exactly, is a Queen of the Night, anyway? Well, as I see it, a Queen of the Night is the hostess-high-priestess. A nightlife ambassadress. A diva-cheerleader. A woman who gives any party credibility just by popping in. A Queen of the Night has a mission: to have the most fun in the most given situations the most often. To encourage and include everyone in her path to join her in her quest for fun. A popular girl on a popular block in a popular town in a popular country in a popular world. Fame breeds more fame. Fame attracts the famous. Then famous fun. And soon you are the legendary Queen of the Night.

By some weird fated and lucky accident, that's just how it happened to me. When I first came to New York City, from Tampa, after my year in London, everyone was long on cool. I was different. Big-boobed. Bouyant. Pneumatic. Happy to be in a place where being called "extreme" and "unique" was a compliment, I was not embarrassed to show my excitement. I smiled! I beamed! I approached everyone, thrilled to be meeting such incredible new people.

So I got noticed. By poets, writers, deejays, artists, rock stars, actors, fashion designers, and the all-important star doormen—you know, the glitterati of swingin' downtown. Eventually, I caught the eye of the White Knight of the Night—the handsome hurricane and New York club impressario Rudolf—and he and I became the Ambassador and Ambassadress of Clubdom. I made friends with friends and friends of friends. My status continued to escalate.

Paparazzi started snapping me. I turned up in the glam columns. I began hosting dinner parties at clubs, with celebrity guest lists. All the famous—and all the famous for being famous—were invited. And showed up. Andy Warhol, for one, who said, "Wow. The greatest party I've ever been to was Dianne Brill's Coffee Achievers birthday party." And it *was* a great bash, complete with gorge, glittering babes dressed only in giant coffee cups and stilettos and the Shirelles singing "Happy Birthday, Dianne," (though Rudolf promised to get me Dean Martin!). Around that time Anthony Haden-Guest in *New York* magazine dubbed me "The Queen of the Night." The press picked up on it here and around the globe. The title stuck.

THE FAB 500

Every city has its core-of-cool favorites. These people are the trend-starters and taste-makers. They're insiders, originals, upstarts—and all others you'd love to see undressed! In Tampa, we had the Fab 15. In New York City, there's the Fab 500. Here's the math: In a city of nine and a half million, there are three thousand favorites. The rising-fringe favorites (the ever-changing new arrivals), outer-circle favorites (almost there), inner-circle favorites (more established), and, finally, the cream-of-the-favorites, the Fab 500.

As one of the Brill Babe Brigade, you are an honorary member of the Fab 500—wherever you happen to live—and the focal point of your own hometown core-of-cool. You are one of the incredible, excitable, and almost unspeakably fabulous! The roots of any self-respecting city's self-promoter's dream.

Once you're part of this inner sanctum, you're one wiggle away from becoming the Queen of the Night, the one favorite-favorite of the favorites! Being Queen of the Night, however, is a *commitment*. A fun job . . . but somebody's *got* to do it! So, Angel Face, why not you?

RULES FOR THE RULER

As the Queen of the Night, you are a cheerleader. Your happy, let's-have-fun emotional state must be consistent in the public eye. You should *not* go out if you don't meet the full life-of-the-party requirements. If you're *out*, you have a commitment to being *on*. Say you don't feel that you have much to give, or you're in a "stank" mood, stay home, because when you're the Queen of the Night, people rely on you to bring them up.

1 You must be prepared to attend all important highlife and lowlife parties on the same night.
2 Here's an RSVP strategy for times when you want to decline but still get invited again, or say yes but leave a loophole so you can get out of it (in case something or someone even more fun comes along): Say, "I'd love to come, though I'll be really late," or, if it's a large dinner party, "I'd love to come for dessert." Then, if you show or don't show, no one will inconvenienced.
3 You must make everyone at his or her moment with the Queen feel like he or she is the most important person in the room to you. Mean it—the eyes tell! Believe me, that's the hard part. Honesty and enthusiasm must rule your reign.
4 Be polite, never mean or cruel, to drunks or creeps. You'll have best results using old-style manners. The most textbook-absurd talk works best. Like: "Ah, you seem to me to be such a gentleman, not so *rude*. Please excuse me, we'll talk another night when you're more yourself."
5 Don't slip into gratuitous "name dropping." This boring trait is not good form for the formidable Queen of the Night.
6 When hosting a party *always* over-invite. Too many is forever better than not enough!
7 When you're the hostess and you greet a new guest that you like, immediately ask him/her: "Okay. Tell me. Would you like to meet anyone here? Anyone. Just tell me." Then be true to your word and introduce him/her to Matt Dillon. Nick Cage. Adam Ant. Debbie

Harry. Grace Jones. Robert Palmer. Simon Le Bon. Nick Rhodes.

8 The dreaded "Do you remember me?" situation is bound to occur. Often. Very often. Especially in a major metroplitan area. There are several ways this can come up. There's the "I'm the friend of so-and-so" whom you probably don't remember either. In that case, ask "Oh! How is so-and-so?" It's likely that he'll slip you some info inadvertently; if not, smile and say "You're great!" Or there's the straight-on "Do you remember me?" confrontation. Immediately reply, "Yes . . ." Look quizzical. "When was the last time we saw each other?" Another tactic is to answer a question with a question, never a flat-out yes or no. Say: "What have you been up to lately?" And in real moments of doubt, try: "Your hair's different." When it's someone you don't recognize but who looks familiar and nice, make up an on-the-spot nickname for him: "Hi, Shoulders!" Which is probably more interesting than Dick, or whatever his real name is.

9 Handle "uncompliments" with your usual charm. Always give the person the benefit of the doubt and assume he or she really means to flatter you no matter how naff the comment comes out. So, when someone says, "Gawd! How much weight did you lose? A hundred pounds!" Don't chant your statistics in this case; just turn it around and say, "Thank you! You look great too!" and keep moving, head toward your next target.

10 When refusing any request—drugs, drink, a casual marriage proposal, whatever—always smile, touch the person's arm and say: "No, of course not!" in the most good-humored tone you've got—and then leave.

11 If a GG you know is standing with a date, always say hello to her immediately after greeting GG . . . or simultaneously if you can. She must not feel excluded or alienated by your royal command. If any GG is with a date, he is *off limits* tonight to every other woman.

There must be a simpatica relationship between you and your fellow babes! The Queen of the Night is loved and respected by both sexes.

12 Like it or not, you are always the host, no matter who is hosting a particular event. As Queen of the Night, you're a cross between a diva and a den mother. People will depend on your clout—and will seek you out even if you're in the middle of a smooch, schmooze, or photo-op, with cries of "Dianne! Please! Help me! I lost my coatcheck ticket and now they won't give me my coat! Will you please talk to them?" or "My date's stuck outside and they won't let him in! Could you please tell the doorman he's cool?" or "Can I have some comp drink tickets?"

PARTYSPEAK

Partyspeak—or party patter—gives you the ability to talk to anyone at any time about anything. Party patter is casual conversation, and the obvious choices are to be real, deep, or superficial. However, being really, deeply superficial is the most useful partyspeak option. It's the thinking babe's small talk. It eliminates the conditioned dull, fake, polite conversation, allowing the freedom of absurdity . . . optimal, because the object of the party game is to have fun.

But is it possible to be real, deep, and superficial simultaneously? Yes. You're being real because you're showing your true fun nature . . . nothing phony about you, babe. The deep part comes from your total belief in, and commitment to, whatever it is you're talking about—that's the hook. And the superficiality factor is the gloss—the hairdo and makeup of your patter, what makes it extra enticing. The three components are layered and intertwined. You really are being deep, real, and superficial at once. Here's the setup: The Queen of the Night is walking through a crowded room. She spies an interesting-looking stranger-babe she wants to talk to.

QUEEN OF THE NIGHT (*a.k.a., you, giving the stranger babe's outfit an approving once-over*): Wow! Right?
STRANGER-BABE (*confused*): Hunh?
QN: When you dance in that, how do you keep the maribou trim from getting moist?
SB: Moist? What do you mean, like, sweaty?
QN: Come on. Babes don't sweat. They shine! Like we're shining now.
SB (*flattered, but still confused*): Yeah . . . right . . . shining.
QN (*in a sisterly conspiracy, low voice*): So. Did you see that strapping specimen leaning against the pillar? I bet if he moved one inch this whole building would collapse.
SB (*relaxed laughter*): Uh oh! He *is* moving.
QN: Well, that's our cue to check out the back room, hmm? So, anyway, where was I? Oh, yeah, my best friend just moved to the Land of the Midnight Sun and . . . Well, there's a party tonight after this where the men outnumber the women two to one. I was going solo, but . . . do you want to come?

Now, let's analyze that little snippet. The *realness* comes from the Queen's genuine desire to form a female alliance with the stranger-babe. The *deepness* comes from the instant intimacy created between the two. The *superficialness*, obviously, is the subject matter—clothes and guys.

In general, being really, deeply superficial as a conversation-starter, just go for an innocuous yet original statement, question, or compliment. Always keep it positive: The reaction you want is laughter or at least a smile. But that's not enough to grab someone's attention. You want to say something cute and funny, yet also a little confusing, so the smile or laugh comes with an inquisitive second look (Huh? Ha!). Remember, people are out because they want to feel good; your purpose is to make the good better—even if it's only momentary.

Let's take a look at some partyspeak do's and don'ts.

PARTYSPEAK DO'S & DON'TS

Don't	Do
Where'd you buy that designer jacket?	Why'd you buy that ALIA jacket? It looks so gorge on you, now I can't wear mine.
I love this song.	This song makes me want to one-two-cha-cha-cha.
Ugh! That huge disco ball is terribly out of style.	Oh, look! A huge disco ball! How flawlessly out of style!
Do you know where the bathroom is?	Does this place really have a Jacuzzi? Where?

PARTYVISION

Why? I don't know but it's a known fact that all Queens of the Night have notoriously poor eyesight. This creates a real challenge because when you're out, you're constantly surrounded by people you know, think you know, should know, want to know, as well as people who think they know or want to know you. Plus, there are the factors of smoke and steam that cloud most clubs—a contact lens wearer's nightmare. Lacking the visual skill, a lot of new senses and techniques naturally develop:

1 To anyone who says hello to you or looks at you with recognition (head still, brows raised, face in your direction), or whose outline or blur of style seems familiar, wave and say "Hey!" "Hi!" or point your finger and say "Wow!" The worst that can happen is that you simply appear

friendly. If they don't know you, let *them* try to figure out when you've never met.

2 A psychic club vision develops with a lot of exposure. You can clock a room in a moment and establish where are the best GGs, celebs, and your favorite trendies. They become your pointed stop-off targets.

3 Too many close faces and bodies can at times become overwhelming. Simply squint your eyes and blur out everything in the room except your immediate circular perimeter. Don't worry. GGs and fab babes will come to you as long as you keep smiling to the music.

4 Scents never lie. You'll learn to identify people, if not by their faces then by their personal fragrances, which always become more pronounced as the party heat rises. This doesn't only apply to perfumes and colognes: I know a guy, a leather designer, whose approach I always sense by the unmistakable essence of tanned hides and just a hint of mothballs.

PARTY TIMING: WHEN BEING LATE IS TOO EARLY

Always be late. The Queen of the Night is always late. You've got to know how late to be for what. There are some occasions where being late is too early. For instance, let's say there's a party that goes from nine to midnight. If you arrive at nine-thirty, a half-hour late, you're too early. You'll be one of the first people there, and you can't make a grand entrance if there's no one there to experience it. By the same token, you don't want to be too late, when the party is winding down. Aim for the peak of the party, in this case, around ten thirty.

The later you are, the better you have to look. If you're going to be very late (unavoidably, not on purpose), your amazing, flawlessly female and perfect appearance is your best excuse. People will take one look at you and know it was worth the wait.

Sometimes people will try to trick you into being on time by telling you a party begins at a ridiculous hour, such as seven thirty. Call a

Virgo, or a Swiss, German, or other Nordic-heritage friend (the species tends to be punctual, for some reason) that you know is invited to the same party and ask them what time he or she is going to be there. Time yourself accordingly.

When a party is going well, you don't want to burn out on it, or have others burn out on you. Do a disappearing act—blend into the fab fringe around the dance floor and watch anonymously; have a lengthy primp-stop in the ladies room; go on to the terrace, balcony, or fire escape. Stay away long enough for people to wonder where you are. Then make a second-wind energetic entrance—it's like going to a whole new party.

Okay, say this party is *over*, as far as you're concerned. How long is polite? Any amount of time, as long as you're sweet and discreet. Exit small (a rule of thumb: grand entrances, minuscule exits). Do not say good-bye. If the host catches you trying to slip out, it's a nightmare. Respect the feelings of your host and give the standby, classic excuse that nobody can argue with: "Thanks so much for inviting me! It's a gorge party. Everybody looks so great. I wish I didn't have to wake up early tomorrow!"

GETTING IN: THE ALL-IMPORTANT FIRST IN

Some secrets about trying to become a club doyenne (you know, like Doyenne Brill):

1. Get yourself invited to a good party at a good club (ask all your friends, friends of friends, hair-dresser, trendy-boutique salesgirl, anyone you think can get you that first, all-important "first in").
2. Overdress, of course, but make sure it's appropriate to the club. You'll have wasted a good five and a half hours preparing yourself if your outfit is not what's right at this particular venue. Think sex-glamma—always a good choice.
3. Approach the doorperson from the perimeter—don't try to push your way through the crowd but sidle up on one side. Don't pout and look

My "First In" host, performer, NYC's forever star doorman Houii Montauge.

bored or arrogant, and never try to out-important the doorperson. Keep your dignity, please, and remember that the doorperson needs and deserves your respect. Smile, give the doorperson a small hi-sign wave (as if you're already great friends). When he/she lets you in, say thanks and look at him/her. Once inside, find out the doorperson's name from the coatcheck person, and use it appropriately.

4 If you want to get into a club with a tough door policy, go when it's raining. The crowd at the door will be thinner and your chances of gaining entrance quickly will be better.

5 Sometimes sneaky tricks are okay. Like when your name is somehow missing from the guest list and the listbearer is very inexperienced and he's acting like a cartoon doorperson instead of a real one. You know, pretentious, full of himself, the club owner's naff nephew. Here's a cute con you and your best babefriend can try. Go up and announce yourself: "I'm Jane Smith. I'm on the list." While the doorperson scans, your cohort, standing on his other side, sneaks a peak at the list. Stall the doorperson and say, "Maybe I'm under *J*." When he informs you that you're not on the list, your pal pipes up: "Maybe they put it under my name, Jane," and offers the name she spied. Boom! You're in.

6 If you ever feel intimidated by the glamosity of all the new "beautiful persons," listen to the Brill: Look at everyone and find something about them that is familiar to you, a common thread or detail that is like you. Such as: Gee, they're all breathing in and out, just like me! Focus on the familiar, not the unfamiliar.

7 Introduce yourself to the host. (Remember: Shyness is the greatest form of conceit.) Compliment the party, its theme, the beauty of the crowd. Chances are that he or she will invite you to the next event. Give your address for the mailing list.

8 Treat all staff members—from the promoter to the barback—with energy, enthusiasm, and courtesy. Forget this cooler-than-thou act; it's not modern and it certainly isn't social.

9 Hit clubs on off nights. This better acquaints you with the staff and establishes you as a regular.

10 If you want to succeed as Queen of the Night tonight, it's Perrier all the way as I do or watch your champagne intake. A Queen is never drunk or sloppy.

11 Above all HAVE FUN!

STEPHEN SABAN
& JOHN SEX
DEBBIE HARRY
PHOTO: PATRICK MCMULLEN
THIERRY MUGLER
RUDOLF & DRINK
TICKET
PHOTO: ROXANNE LOWIT
BIRTHDAY BOY SPROUSE
ADAM ANT
BRILL'ANT
PINUP
PARTY
TOUKIE SMITH, FELLOW
ROOTSTEIN MANNEQUIN
ANDY, APPLE & BRILL
ME SINGING "HAPPY
BIRTHDAY" IN NEW YORK CITY
ME, MY MAN &
SUZANNE
PHOTO:
PATRICK
MCMULLEN

LISA SLIWA

JOEY ARIAS "DALI" & ME BACKSTAGE

JANIS SAVITT:
IT'S MARACA TIME!

FILMING AN "ART AGAINST AIDS" VIDEO

MATT DILLON WITH BRILL BURNS-
DON'T WORRY
WE'RE REALLY
ONLY JUST
FRIENDS, DAMMIT!

PETER
& ME IN
PARIS

A QUEEN OF
THE NIGHT:
SUZANNE
BARTSCH

ALIX MALKA / PHOTO: ROXANNE LOWIT

MUSCLE MUSIC &
HUMAN CHANDELIERS

PHOTO: PATRICK MCMULLEN

BRAD, BRILL &
MY MENTORIC
MUGLER

NICK RHODES

NICK CAGE IN WHAT USED TO BE DEAN
MARTIN'S CAR IN THE SIXTIES

BOY GEORGE,
ME & A
(!*?) GG

ACTRESS DEB MAZAR, DANILO & "CONNIE GIRL"

KOHLE YOHANNAN &
MARY MCFADDEN

JULIE RHODES & M.C. LOLA

DREAM GODDESS DOLLY PARTON

PHOTO: PATRICK MCMULLEN

CHRISTIE BRINKLEY

GENTLE LEGEND, ARTIST KEITH HARING

ZANDRA RHODES & MICHAEL SOUTHGATE

RODNEY DANGERFIELD BACKSTAGE AFTER FILMING HBO SPECIAL

MUGLER

WRITER STEPHEN SABAN

MY DEVILISH BILLY BOY

PHOTO: ROXANNE LOWIT

FAWNLIKE SABINA STREETER

RUDOLF & YELLO'S DIETER MEIER

A QUEEN OF THE NIGHT & BEST FRIEND ANITA SARKO & PHIL DONAHUE

SIMON LE BON SHARING MY ACCESSORIES

NICK RHODES & STEPHEN SPROUSE

MICHAEL MUSTO, JAMES ST. JAMES & FRIENDS

PHOTO: PATRICK MCMULLEN

IMAN & NAOMI

PHOTO: ROXANNE LOWIT

HALLOWEEN: THE PONY GIRL

THE DIFFERENT TYPES OF FUN

Fun is my operative. My fuel. But there are a lot of kinds of fun:

Boring Fun

Boring fun is no fun until afterward. Like a black-tie benefit dinner for some admirable but boring charity with a Las Vegas legend as the chairman. The guests include, say, Dean Martin (of course), Frank Sinatra, maybe Shirley MacLaine, and every society matron in town. It's at a grand hotel banquet room for six hundred people, with the table squad serving the same chicken dinner they serve at every banquet (be it fifty dollars or five thousand dollars a plate). This *should* be fun, with the glamorous old crowd of Hollywood-Vegas-New York. But no. They get on stage, make a couple of textbook banquet jokes—no fantastic routines, no dancing or even chanting, and doll, where the hell's "New York, New York." A party where nothing happens. Then, the next day, when your friends ask you: Who was there? What was she wearing? Was he drunk? What does his toupee look like up close? Can you see any face-lift scars? How many diamonds? How was "New York, New York"? Then, when you start to explain last night with these kinds of questions, it starts to be fun. The more you remember, the more fun it is. In a week's time, looking back, it seems like the party of the year.

Fast Fun

Boom, boom, boom. A party, a gallery opening, a dinner, a fashion show, a bar, a bistro, a bowling alley . . . do 'em all, do 'em fast, do 'em in one night. The object of this game is to keep moving. Action. Activity. Speed. Don't stop until after-after-hours.

To have fast fun, you must adopt my *peak of the party theory:* Hit it at its peak, when the fun is at its extreme, highest height. Kiss and hello all your favorites; order a drink while clocking the room to see if there's anyone you've neglected to dazzle or be dazzled by. Then, just as you feel the energy start to drop slightly from its fever pitch, disappear. Your timing is perfect. You've left, things wind down, and to everyone around you made the party. It was high when you were there, it went flat when you were gone, thus enhancing your reputation for giving instant fast fun credibility to any event.

Be sure to take at least one person with you from each spot so that you accrue a crew. Also crucial to fast fun: sunglasses. When all night long your flame burned twice as brightly, and twice as fast, the early morning light could blow your glam image,—the least you can do is protect your sanity by shielding your eyes.

Out of the cab. Kisses and good-byes. Now feel the satisfaction that you were at the right place at the right time all the time tonight.

Serious Fun

Also known as Intellectual Fun. This is the most challenging kind of fun. Basically, it's an established avant-garde art opening, ballet soirée, book party—someplace where a lot of highbrow, art-hungry, or academic types are gathered. At first glance, everyone seems to be parading intelligence and connections—a party where everyone talks and no one listens. You'll also find at these events a number of people trapped inside an antisocial shell. They're all trying to be terribly grown up!

Truth is, they're dying to have fun! All they need is the spark—you—to get them going. You walk in. Aaah! a breath of fresh air. Visually, in your overdressed state, you're stimulating. Just start making totally trivial conversation—about your favorite new cartoon character, for instance. Don't muffle your laughter. Should someone give you an icy, ghastly glance, return the look with your warmest smile and melt that person on the spot. Ask him or her a partyspeak question like: "Who do you think is more internationally famous: Solzhenitsyn or Brigitte Bardot?" In other words, treat this stuffy affair as you would any other high-profile fun event. People will love you! They'll relax; their shells will crack; and by the time you make your exit, they'll be fighting over who gets to wear the lampshade on his head!

Foreign Fun

Communications complications notwithstanding, this can be one of the most fun kinds of fun! It can come in several forms. You're trotting the globe, you're entertaining foreign friends, or you sashay up to a group of gorgeous GGs and discover they're all Greek or Antarctican or from some other exotic land. In any of these sitches, rely on international symbols and gestures. For instance, say you're doing the Pocket Square Exchange with a handsome foreign gentleman. Make sure he "gets it" by the mirth in your eyes and the sexy way your hands move in and around his pocket. Do a modernized version of the "Me Jane, You Tarzan" thing. If all techniques fail, rely on the internationally understood language of the kiss.

That takes care of when they are where you are. But what about when you are where they are? When traveling to a foreign country, what are the first words you want to learn in this tongue . . . after the dirty ones and the all-important phrase "One espresso, please"? Sure, you're probably ambitious, with your Berlitz course handbook in your handbag; but it's no simple feat to master a foreign language overnight. For instance, did you know that the rooster's "cock-a-doodle-do" doesn't even sound like our phonetic "cock-a-doodle-do" in a foreign language? Get this, babes:

German: "Kee-ka-rik-kee"
Italian: "Chee-chee-reechee"
Japanese: "Coke-a-loke-ko"

With all these cultural differences, how are you ever going to have any foreign fun? Well, the only word you really need to learn how to say properly is *yes*. *Yes* guarantees adventure . . . in any lingo or any land.

Here's how to say *yes* in French, one of my favorite languages and the one that is most universally romantic. Of course we know that "yes" in French is *oui* (whee). What is important, *ma petite poupée*, is that we observe the *way* to say *oui*. In English, when we say "yesssssss," notice that the breath comes *out* of our lovely mouths, while in French, our breathy "wheeeeeee" must be sucked in, creating a round, persuasive, Frenchie pout. The Frenchie pout is of the utmost importance in the French language. Try this exercise to prepare for *oui*—it will put your mouth in an automatic Frenchie pout and you'll be appropriately out of breath. Start slowly. Say out loud: "Bo-Bo-Bo-Bo-Bo." Increase! Faster! "Bo-Bo-Bo-Bo-Bo!" Now decrease speed. "Bo. Bo. Bo. Bo. Bo." Now say it! "Wheeeeee": You got it! Welcome to fun with a foreign language.

THE SOCIAL DONUT THEORY

Social donuts are little cliques or circles of friends. Some small, some big. They make up every nightlife environment. And like all good donuts, there's cream in the center. Your goal, as Queen of the Night, is to form a delicious social donut around yourself. Here's how:

Me "tasting" the cream from the social donut.

1 Make a grand entrance. The entrance to a club or larger party is different from any other entrance because of the crowd factor. You must make sure nobody misses your arrival. If people are going in before you, wait; you need space—six feet in front of you, at least. Deep breath, think grand, squeeze your butt muscles so you stand high. Pause an instant at the threshold,

then walk in s-l-l-l-o-o-o-w-l-y yet sweepingly. Smile. Cocky-frivolous, like you just heard something really funny and smart. Look directly at the back wall, not at the people in front of you. Clock the perimeter of the room, moving from the left corner to the right. (It's a stage-acting device: Everyone will think you're looking right at them . . . and they'll want to share the source of your smile.)

2 Do a friendly blanket flirt (women and men) of the territory. You'll see what social donuts have already formed. Make a baby grand entrance at the section of the room you want to start in.

3 Float over to the nearest, most interesting donut. Make a micro-entrance into this donut, tossing frivolous and fascinating questions and compliments around. Now, the cream of this particular donut is indeed into being the cream, so you don't want to obviously steal this person's thunder. The idea is to show the cream that he or she can have even more fun with you and bring along whomever he or she wants. Eventually, the cream will respond to one of your questions, and at that point SEDUCE! SEDUCE! SEDUCE! That means focusing totally on the cream for a few minutes. The cream will respond and want to tell you more and more. At that moment, withdraw your attention ever so slightly, then return it to the cream. He or she will be even more intent upon you. Then suggest an introduction into another donut.

4 At the next donut, the cool quotient of you and your "stolen cream" or "tasted cream" will seduce the center of that donut. There's always someone who wants to meet someone.

5 Keep moving from donut to donut, "tasting" the centers away from each one. See what's happening? You're forming the ultimate social donut around the creamiest cream there is—you doll.

6 Maintain awareness of what else is going on in the room. Once you've got a large, exciting social donut built, you can feel free to shout out to anyone you spy, so he or she can join your circle.

7 Eventually, all this elitism vanishes because of the sheer size and volume of your donut. The cream is surrounded by the cream which becomes more cream which merges into all cream. In other words, the entire party is one creamy social donut of your creation.

BEING A SLASH-PERSON

So far, all this Queen of the Night stuff has been party, party, party. Now, let's talk about how you can use nightlife to open daylife doors. Stephen Sprouse, an artist/designer friend of mine, and I came up with a term over dinner one night: *slash-person*. A slash-person is a person with multiple careers. Dancer/sculptor/publicist—that's a three-slash career babe. Modern persons, especially but not limited to those in creative fields, are slash-persons. And, the more multifaceted you are, the easier it is to plug in to different people in a social setting. You're not "networking" (p.u.!) or looking for "connections"; it's not a matter of what *they* can do for *you*, but what you can do together.

Of course you can be successful in lots of projects. The secret is to make sure they all interconnect in some way, so one helps to promote the other. For instance, say you're a nightclub performer who's also a jewelry designer: wear your jewelry on stage. If you're a secretary and do catering as a side project, cater a company party and use every moment to promote future food jobs.

So, you know you can have as many careers as you want. How do you know *which* careers you want? Saddle up a stable of stallions and see which one(s) you enjoy riding most. When you were a little girl, what was it that you wanted to be when you grew up? Does that idea still hold any appeal to you? If yes, try it. Secretly at first—you don't have to make your aspiration public until you're comfortable with it.

What about when someone suggests a career that never even entered your mind? Like, "These snapshots are great! Have you ever thought about becoming a photographer?" Give it a shot, babe!

A NEW YORK MOMENT

MIRIAM SCHAFER

DESIGNER RIFAT OZBEK IN LONDON

RUPERT EVERETT

LAWRENCE MONOSON & THIERRY MUGLER

HELLOOOO: TELEPURRING IN PUBLIC

MY BEST FRIEND JANIS SAVITT

PARISIAN NIGHTLIFE KING CLAUDE CHALLE

ACTOR IAN BUCCANAN

MY BIG LITTLE SISTER MORRI

MARIE SEZNEC OF CHRISTIAN LACROIX FAME & I DO SOFIA & JAYNE

WITH QUENTIN CRISP & ACTRESS SYLVIA MILES

DAVID LEE ROTH

PHOTO: PATRICK MCMULLEN

LINDA EVANGELISTA

PHOTO: ROXANNE LOWIT

NICK RHODES

J.P.G. & PHOTOGRAPHER PIERRE RUTCHIE

PHOTO: PATRICK MCMULLEN

ROBERT PALMER

ME & JEAN-PAUL "BAT" GAULTIER IN NYC

BOY GEORGE

ME & NICK BEWIGGED

ANDY WARHOL & JEAN-MICHEL BASQUIAT / PHOTO: PATRICK MCMULLEN

ME IN THE CONVERTIBLE NIGHTLIFE KING RUDOLF ALWAYS PROMISED ME

SANDRA BERNHARD: ANGEL IN A WHITE DRESS

DAVID LETTERMAN BACKSTAGE AFTER I DID HIS SHOW

PHOTO: PATRICK MCMULLEN

RUDOLFO THE MAGNIFICENT

DURAN DURAN'S JOHN TAYLOR & NICK RHODES

PETER & I GO TO THE OPERA HOUSE IN GERMANY

JON WEISER & ADEL ROOTSTEIN HERSELF

JANIS SAVITT

HUBERT "MR. PARIS" & AMANDA LEAR / PHOTO: ROXANNE LOWIT

BEAUTY IS GRACE JONES

Maybe you're inspired by something you've seen in a movie or read in an autobiography. Whatever . . . try it. Don't limit yourself, and that means time-wise, too. *There is no time limit to "Making It."*

Avoid the company of naysayers. Surround yourself with equally creative, ambitious, supportive people. Nightlife environments nurture this kind of creative support system. Even competition can be healthy if you let it spur you on—just be sure that you *never judge other slash-persons' accomplishments as your failures.* You and your circle of will-bes should promote and applaud each other's career ventures. But bear in mind that while your allies may help you, they won't "make" you—so you must believe that *you* are the best promoter of *you* in the world.

Self-Promotion: Doin' It Right

1 When someone says, "Hey! How are you?" do not immediately recite your resume and your past, present, and future projects. This is something we tend to do in NYC and L.A. . . . but it's not answering the question. Now, if someone asks you "*What* are you doing?" that's your cue to self-promote. But do it with subtlety. And if you happen to be in between projects, throw the question back on them, quickly: "What's going on with you?"

2 Promote *basically* honestly. Exaggerate, but don't overexaggerate your projects. Hyper-hype can backfire on you.

3 Be patient: Don't reveal too much about pending projects. It's okay to give them a tease, though: "Something really interesting could happen—I don't know yet, but it's great." Be sure to tell everyone: "You'll be the first to know when it happens!" It's simply a question of pacing . . . give them a little info and they'll want to know more.

4 When talking about yourself and your accomplishments, be proud but not pompous. Never talk down to anyone, ever, because that person could be in a position to help you some day. Arrogance gets you nowhere.

5 One of the best ways to get people to help you is to help them.

6 Know when *not* to talk. As a well-known Babe Buddy once told me: "Never do a talk show if you have nothing to promote at the time." Why? Because you're setting yourself up for victimization. Especially if you're sexy (and you are!). "At first the public will applaud sexuality and be drawn to it. But then the public will have to punish the object, because being overtly sexy is ultimately against Puritan society." It's great to be sexy, but you are not a sex object. Use your sexiness and everything else about you—your quirkiness, your sense of humor, your pain-in-the-assedness—to promote. But when you have nothing to say, say nothing.

7 Train your voice to be directed, enthusiastic, cheerful, but with a professional, polite edge. Never shriek—even in a noisy club environment. If you have something interesting to say, people will hush up and get closer to you in order to hear it.

8 Don't think of it as a signature, think of it as an autograph. Change yours if it doesn't look strong and important. Check out my signature before and after signings:

Dianne Brill Dianne Brill

9 What are the six most important words in self-promotion? *Thank you! Thank you! Thank you!*

Health Tips for the Queen of the Night

The Queen of the Night has to keep her strength up and her energy high.

1 The best dietary supplements for a night on the town are vitamins B12 (energy) and E (sexiness) and ginseng (extra-sexy energy).

2 Be sure to eat a light healthy meal for stamina before going out to a party that has a buffet. The food at the spread will no doubt be tempting (probably something trendy-ethnic), but bean breath is not a socially seductive smell.

3 "Disco nap"! If you went out the night before, and you're going out again tonight, girl, you got to have your disco nap! Lights out and fit in a snooze sometime during your five-and-a-half-hour dressing/primping schedule. (Sleep on your back so as not to puff your eyes or harm your hairdo.)

4 When you get overheated from dancing, don't stand in front of the AC—you could catch a chill. Go into the ladies room and apply cool water to your pulsepoints, forehead, and back of the neck. If you can't get to a sink, do this with ice cubes. But remember, make it a performance.

5 It's difficult to avoid an onslaught of cigarette smoke when you're at a party, but there are subtle ways to keep people from blowing it directly in your face. Try saying, "You look just like an old-time Hollywood movie star with that cigarette in your mouth. Let's see it in profile. Oh, perfect! Stay that way!"

6 Once a week, do a lock-in. You've just come back from a fabulous, incredible, late Saturday night—the culmination of a week's worth of celebrations—and you're gorgeously, happily exhausted. Tired, but fulfilled. Now you need to recuperate, recover, and recharge your beautiful batteries, babe. Lock the door and don't leave till Monday morning. Do everything slowly and self-indulgently. Don't work or even think about work. Don't do anything you don't want to. This is totally mindless time. *Loll, doll!* Acceptable activities for the lock-in include love espionage on the phone, sleeping, watching videos, nibbling things that will restore depleted magnesium reserves (spinach or chocolate, take your pick). You will emerge on Monday refreshed, alive, ambitious, and ready for the coming week's hard work of fun.

Loll, Doll!

MICHEL COMTE

Deeply pondering the cosmic complexities & philosophical significance of getting dressed in "just under six hours."

CHAPTER 8

How to Get Dressed in Just Under Six Hours

When I'm out on the runway, cha-cha-cha-ing, sashaying, and shimmying, I'm living a glamma-girl, Barbie-doll fantasy. Sometimes I think back to the Saturday afternoons of my early babehood. My mom, Noni, used to buy old bridesmaids' dresses and junk jewelry for me and my babe-ettes to play with. Di Davidson, Patti Vesallo, Lilly Martinez, and I would spend our six hours dressing up as Queen of the World and Millie the Model. Well, you have total little-girl-woman excitement when playing grown-up designer dress-up on the runway.

I have advantages because modeling is one of my many "jobs" or "projects," so I'm *in* the model universe but not *of* it. I come and I go, on to the next project, so modeling doesn't get boring . . . and I don't have to play by any of the model rules. I'm just Dianne Brill, sort of like (as writer and friend Stephen Saban says) a commercial break in between the traditional catwalk chi-chi babes.

I've survived some perils in my *défilé* life. Like the time Thierry Mugler, the tall, handsome, totally sexy genius (after all, he discovered me—for the runway, anyway) clothing designer flew me to Paris to appear as the climax of his show. Thierry put me in his magnificent wedding gown. Then he put me on a motorized swing. One hundred and ten feet in the air. With no net. I was to descend from the ceiling, accompanied by thousands of pink and white balloons, with "The Girl Can't Help It" playing from the loudspeakers, then land on stage and toss my wedding bouquet.

Backstage, the motorized switch run by a stagehand who only spoke French held my fate. Before the curtain went up, the switch got stuck! I was moving heavenward, inches from a huge group of glaring spotlights. I screamed at the stagehand in English, but from his perspective he couldn't see my danger. Finally, "*Putain! Arrêt! Arrêt*!" (translation: Nasty name! Stop! Stop!) magically came from my mouth. He understood—just six inches before my body would have met the hot lights, leaving me a fried bride. The show was an overwhelming success, without a hair out of place on my blonde, be-falled head.

That traumatic episode might have frightened some babes away from modeling forever. But not this babe. I dared tempt fate again. My next infamous incident has been called "The Babe Who Fell to Earth." Or was it to worth? Was I a fallen woman? Acrobat? Or accident? You be the judge! So here's how it went. . . .

Mugler, who had shown me off for years in his extravaganzas de la mode and had become a strong influence on my look on and off stage, wanted me for an upcoming collection. Of course, I said yes. My friendship, my alliance, runs deep to him; and he, like all designers—is extremely possessive of his discoveries. But that very same season, I was also asked to be a special guest in Jean-Paul Gaultier's show. Negotiations behind the scenes were touchy, but a deal was finally struck—no hard feelings. Yes, I could do my *défilé de Paris* in both shows without being an unfaithful woman. Aah!

Moments before falling to worth.

So, guilt-free, I started my fittings for Gaultier. Jean-Paul is one of those quirky, hunky type GGs who completely realizes that though he looks like a grown-up he is really the *enfant terrible* who rages wild and happy behind his eyes. So if he says: "You're so grandiose! You are my beautiful *Mademoiselle Bon Bon de Paris*, Brill," even when I'm wearing his bloomer trousers, sailor shirt, butch army boots (with HHs, *bien sur*), and umbrella to match, I *had* to believe the little boy's vision.

It began! Six thousand people from around the world fought chic-to-chic to enter the Halle de la Villette—a slaughterhouse made of glass—where the show was being held. Lots of my friends—fab and some famous, such as Grace Jones and Boy George—were in the crush. Backstage, it was typical organized madness. I call it assembly-line beauty—being "prepared" for nearly six hours by countless hair stylists, makeup artists, and dressers. Amid the mayhem, some babes were dishing about all the VIPs in the audience, particularly Jack Nicholson, who was right in the front row.

(Well, every time I hear this guy's name—though, truly, I never had a "thang" for him—I have to laugh to myself. I've only met him twice, and both times he *ran* from me. The first time was at Mick Jagger and Jerry Hall's place in New York—a small party for twenty-five people or so, casual, intimate. Mick and Jerry ruled. Jack was nice enough. But soon after our introduction, I burned him with someone else's cigarette, spilled some food on his shirt, and drizzled Perrier on his foot. The guy avoided me all evening after that—which was not easy in the two-room party section of the apartment. Let's say, due to some odd, unexplainable circumstances, my charisma didn't shine for Jack.

The second time I was introduced to him was at the Palladium, a then-important NYC nightclub, by Andy Warhol. In seconds, by some weird accident, my Perrier was once again in his shoes. This time I laughed, and Jack quickly disappeared. It was a bad comedy. I hoped, for *his* sake, I'd never fall into this guy's company again.)

But I hear you, babes: "Just tell us what happened in the Gaultier show, Brill!" Okay! The stage was about ten feet high. Large, and the shape of a racetrack, with rounded edges. Photographers were in the center and all around the edges of the stage. Backstage we were all dressed and ready. I was mesmerized by how every babe looked so gorge. We were an army! And as the special guest of the show, I was ready to rage and rule! We all made our passages, minding our HH army boots near the rounded edges of the stage. The crowd was alive and really cheered us on. All *my* friends had the biggest mouths—thank God!

My second-to-last passage came. I was loving the audience, loving the clothes, and was just so happy being there. All of a sudden I was inspired to take on a backwards maneuver. The lights bright, paparazzi cameras flashing, and all I heard was six thousand people at once hold their collective breath: "Aaaaaaah!" My heart stopped. I was balanced on the very edge of the ten-foot-high stage. Time froze, like in a car crash when you're just about to collide. Was I going to fall from grace, lose control, and land in a certainly humiliating fashion on my broken butt off the catwalks of Paris? Or was I going to stay on the runway and continue my hoochie-koochie walk?

I didn't know what was next, right? But in that time-freeze, I thought of my sister, Morri, who in times of need always repeats our family motto: "If there's a Brill, there's a way!" I decided not to risk attempting to balance back on the edge of the stage but to go with the jump and control it. Well, God's hand glided me off the stage and I gracefully landed on my HHs like an Olympic star. I held my hands over my head—a 9.5 landing, I thought, if this were the Olympics. The crowd went wild. WILD! Screaming, clapping, yelling! I climbed back up on the runway to finish my walk. This was a real time-marking moment for me. The Catwalk Queen always lands on her feet.

P.S. Oh. And guess who's front-row lap I barely missed falling into? Yep! That's right! Jack Nicholson's!

ALVARO
FLASH
Lights bright,
paparazzi flashing . . .

ne froze . . .
My olympic-gold-
medal 9.5 landing!

EVERYBABE BEAUTY: TRUTH FROM DIANNE BRILL, YOUR SIREN OF STYLE

It's true. These are good times for looking good. Every babe is beautiful. Because every kind of face is in the "in" column. Every kind of hair and feature placement is attractive. I've seen, on magazine pages, movie screens, and Paris runways, women with noses shaped in the most marvelous ways. All the things we were teased about in junior high school, from hair to foot, are now our beauty strengths. And these girlies are gorgeous. Elegant. Stunning. Model role models.

And bodies? Rounder—absolutely. All boobs? Yes, in every shape. Firm legs and butts—still (goddammit)—but in any and every size. Heavy ankles? Yep. Thin ankles? Yep. Thin legs? Yep. Curvy legs? Them, too. Big feet? Beaucoup! Knock knees? Yep. Weight fluctuation? Yeah, yeah, yeah.

Women looking female. Women using all face and body *uniqueness as assets*, as advantages. Finally, *we* let the fashion designers and the media know what *we* want, as babes, for ourselves and our stars. They're listening!

Be aggressive when it comes to your style. You've got to find it. And keep finding it. Match your outta glamma to your inner glamma. Style is imagination, not dictation. You have to look within, choose what it is that you want to project—your style of the moment. And you have to look around you for influences, inspirations, ideas. Little things, big things, to add and subtract from *your* thing. True style is never stagnant; it's always changing—as spontaneous as it is contrived. Kinda like a true babe! Vanity and realness, heart and heat.

The Lifespan of a Look

In acting, you research a look for a character, a type in a time period, and develop an inner and outer personality to go with it. This often means a drastic reinvention to fit each role. In a more subtle way, in real life, you get the excitement, the newness, the personal impact by regularly reinventing your look.

How long does a look last? Until you get fed up with it. When you catch a glimpse of yourself and something doesn't seem fresh. It's too well rehearsed, too blasé.

Maybe you say "My look is so tired"—and your babe buddies don't give a chorus of "No!" And you start getting compliments like "I have exactly the same light brown outfit!" from people whose taste and fashion sense don't mesh with your own—like those stuck in a catalogue-style coma.

Other signs that it's time for a change? When all of the look's components are prominently displayed in every store window at the nearest mall. When a salesperson in a store tells you "These are selling like hotcakes! We've almost sold out!" (Never, ever buy anything after a pitch like that!)

The best rule of thumb: the minute "style" becomes "fashion"—meaning, everybody's wearing it—it dies. The search for style has taken over the need to be "in fashion." The outcome of fashion is, inevitably, that everyone winds up looking alike. Having real style means accepting an all-over outlook of fashion adaptability—taking the essence of a look you like and personalizing it, showing it in a way that feels good, feels right, on you.

When a look has lost its newness—and *you*ness—it's time to reinvent and adapt until you find your next new look. A new look is a new entrance, a reconjuring of your personal presentation.

Getting a new look does not mean burning everything in your closet and starting from scratch. It can be as simple as changing the part in your hair, brushing on a heavier eyebrow, adding a beauty mark to your cheekbone, undoing a couple of buttons, or wearing a just-long-enough suit jacket without the skirt.

The Great Blonde Hope

Hair and makeup are part of your look and need to be reinvented regularly. It is my opinion that every babe can go blonde at least once. Dye it? Try it! Wig out? Why not! Black, latin, Asian, brown-eyed? Sure.

But bear in mind that going blonde is a commitment (even if only a short-lived one). Changing your shade to red, brunette, or black is work, but the devotion level is much higher for a blonde, because blondness demands attention. One extra-ignored week could cause the neighbor's adorable ten-year-old to approach you as you leave your home with a new GG and say something like: "Why is your hair black there and yellow there, Miss Hollywood?" (Hollywood is what the neighborhood kids all call me.) From the mouths of babes—bab*ies*, not Brill babes—come words so true, they could lead your Berliner-date to say: "You make colorings on your hairs?" "Yes, I'm as natural a blonde as Jayne Mansfield and Marilyn Monroe!" you shoot back. He looks puzzled . . . and relieved, right? (That's because he thinks JM and MM were natural blondes, like so many of his countryfolk.) The word is: No, roots don't rule in a blonde's reality. Unless you're Debbie Harry or the gorgeous Nick Rhodes of Duran Duran, of course, who tells me he likes being blonde, but only with dark roots—in fact, he bleaches the top *and* darkens the roots.

Working Your Assets Off

Before you get dressed, you gotta know what your best assets are and how to play them to the hilt. This has to do with your outward, obvious physical plusses, of course, but more importantly, your inner feelings about sensuous style.

Chances are, you already know what your unique and finest physical assets are. You also know, having developed an appreciation for your U-world, how lingerie can serve where nature may have been a little lax, improving any aspect of your anatomy and making every part of you breathtaking. So working your assets off is about how clothes fit your psyche as much as how they fit your figure.

I know that snug, form-fitting clothes are best for me. Maybe the Empire-waist dress with mile-long sleeves is the ruling rage. I don't care. Sure, some babes look delectable in those swingy little trapeze dresses. But that's simply not my style. I know that I can best realize my Goddess Complex in clothes that cling to my every curve because of the way they make *me* feel. But, within the spectrum of snug, there's a whole lot of variety that can superbly suit all facets of my style personality. Because every babe has a "multiple-style personality."

Style is constantly reinventing yourself. With clothes, makeup, hairstyles, you bring out different aspects of you—the you of the moment. And, babe, you'd be surprised how many women you are! Everything from sweet, darling, adorable angel baby to vixen, villainess, diablesse, and every babe in between—they are alive inside you!

Most of the time you're an irresistible combination of angelic and devilish. Maybe one day you feel a little naughtier; the next, the scales tip toward the sweetness side. Every day, before you put on a stitch of clothing, think about the dramatic duality of your nature and the incredible range in between. Figure out how you feel today and dress the part! You are every woman in one woman and need a full spectrum of style.

Sensual Shopping

Never think of shopping as buying clothes. Think of it as a sensual experience and an exercise in self-expression.

1 Shop in stores that make you feel good because they're "your" places. You find these shops. You get great deals there. They're *your* places, secret style sources to trade with *only* your closest friends.
2 Wear a "do" that won't get too destroyed coming in and out of those

BACKSTAGE WITH JERRY HALL JAGGER, JASMINE LE BON & LINDA EVANGELISTA
MY MUGLER SPACE SUIT LANDED WITH APPLAUSE IN HIS SHOW
PICK A SHOE, ANY SHOE
MASTER DESIGNER MUGLER ADDS TOUCHES TO MY SPACE SUIT
CAROL JOHNSON PREPPING BACK-STAGE
MAKEUP MAGICIAN PAINTS ME TO BEAUTY
IN FOR A FITTING WITH JEAN-PAUL GAULTIER, BUT FIRST A "LAP BREAK"
ME OY GEVALTING WHILE JEAN-PAUL LOOKS ON
CINDY CRAWFORD & NAOMI CAMPBELL
PHOTO: ROXANNE LOWIT
D.B. ON A MAKEUP MISSION
SUPER STYLIST DANILO & ME AS "CRUELLA DEVILLE"
GETTING READY FOR RAQUEL WELCH'S ROCK VIDEO
BACKSTAGE BODY MAKEUP

WHAT A JOB: TAKING CLOTHES ON & OFF BABES ALL DAY

DANILO & ME IN WIG HEAVEN

JEAN-PAUL & MIMI DRESS ME—OOPS!

BACKSTAGE WITH THE FASHION ARMY

ME IN A MUGLER FEATHER WIG WITH MY MAN

BACKSTAGE WITH DANILO: A BRILL DO IN THE MAKING

PETER & ME THE NIGHT I WAS SAVED FROM BEING A FRIED BRIDE

BLACK HAIR BRILL

PHOTO: ROXANNE LOWIT

BRILLBARELLA / PHOTO: ROXANNE LOWIT

THIERRY MUGLER: A DESIGNER IN ACTION

DRESSING WITH A DRESSER BACKSTAGE

peak-clinging turtlenecks two sizes smaller than anything else in the store—and on sale.

3 Experience design, fabric, and color on a totally sensual level. When you look at a dress on a hanger, what kind of emotions do the lines conjure? How do the colors make you feel? Touch the fabric and think of a GG—how will he feel with it against his arm, his hand, his face.
4 Try everything on, and make sure you're wearing the right HHs and U-world.
5 Before looking in the fitting-room mirror, close your eyes and "feel the style." Tickle your fingers over your body. Move around in the dress. Can you envision an army of GGs just dropping to their knees at the sight of you in this creation?
6 Now open your eyes. Drink in the sight of yourself from all angles. Ask yourself: Does this outfit work my assets? Should anything be taken in anywhere? Does it show my spillage adequately? Highlight my heavenly legs? Make the most of my delectable derriere? Feature the face? Show off only the good parts of my parts?

Live the Look

While in the dressing room, imagine yourself out on a date in the outfit you're thinking of buying. Strike a number of poses. My favorites:

1 Hug yourself in slo-mo (slow motion, of course). Drop head, eyes look up, arms wrap your upper body, shmushing spillage to the best advantage. Left shoulder meets your chin. Three-quarter face. Eyes glowing up. Does the mirror love the garment? If not, then "Next!!!"
2 One hand on the hip. With the other hand, pick up the right or left corner of the dress, your best leg thrust forward. Point the toe of the best leg, now spread that leg over with one knee bent, slightly in. Look up, then dooooowwwn. Wrinkle your nose, smilingly baring top row of teeth for one second. Okay. Is this mode "aaaaah-inspiring"? Let's check from behind.

3 Have your derriere facing the mirror. Put your arms over your head, hands crisscrossed on top of hairdo (classic bathing-beauty pose). Push one hip out. Now peek your head through your arms out over your shoulder and gaze into the looking glass. If this outfit doesn't scream out to be bought with full commitment, do more shopping, doll, or go home and whip up a Café Frappé.

RECIPE FOR CAFÉ FRAPPÉ

Ingredients:

- 1 blender, fast speed
- 1 tray ice cubes
- 3 packets artificial sweetener
- 1 tablespoon pure vanilla extract
- ½ blender cool, black, strong coffee

Directions:

Put it in / turn it on / make it smooth / mmmmm! We like it like that, a post-shopping, almost-zero-calorie delight.

Healthy version:

Substitute two tablespoons organically grown honey for Equal, decaf for coffee, ground up natural vanilla bean for extract. Add a splash of soy milk if you like.

BECOMING A CHAMELEON

We're all made up of fifty million things—everyone we know, everything we see, hear, taste, and smell has an effect on us. Use it! You're a collage of different perspectives, a melange of new, often startlingly different ideas that come together and form your unique you-of-the-moment. No matter what style you try on for now, you will always retain your essence.

Look at every look. See something you like? Make it your own. This does not mean copying someone else's style. You do that, you look like a bad imitation of another babe. Take the essence of the style you admire, mingle it with your own inclinations, always with an eye to how this look helps to show you off, doll. In other words, doll: *Chameleon* your new look—*don't clone it.* Besides the women—and even the men—that you see around you every day and night, there are other important sources of style. These are all important reference materials:

Fashion magazines: High-fashion domestic and international are best for fresh, creative, or risk-taking newness in glamma. English mags have the most eccentric new looks. The French are avant as well, and they have that Parisian polish that's a must. Italian *Vogue* is an inspiration—buy it. Any Soviet fashion magazine in your path must be destroyed so as not to influence you in *any way*. . . .

Pick mags that have interesting takes on makeup and hair and that feature the babes and celebs you like. Flip through, pick your type in terms of coloring and shape (close enough), and study her look. While flipping through, you're sure to see a gorge babe, a real "Ms. Natural Resources," who looks as if she just woke up that way. You know. Lock of hair falling perfectly, almost hiding one fluffy-lashy eye. Soft, pearl-finished skin—flawless. Sculptured face with no shine, only nature's rosy glow that flushes her cheek. Lips, perfectly shaped, moist, gently pouted. Ooooh! . . . Wouldn't it be nice to be a babe like that? You'd have everything you always wanted. Well, *you* are that babe—after an internationally famous and very experienced team of hair stylists, makeup artists, lighting assistants, superstarhotshit photographer and fashion designer darling spend their six hours on you. (Soon, we're going to spend those six hours on *you*, so for now it's study time.)

Film books: Check out *all* the Hollywood goddesses, from then to now. Look at the way the blondes, brunettes, and redheads present their hair and faces. Again, pick a type you "sort of" look like or identify with. Figure out what it is you like about their look and how you can work it into your own. Take the photo to your hairdresser, or try to create the coif at home by yourself. Practice makeup techniques—how to get Sophia's cat-eyes, Brigitte's pout, Raquel's bone structure.

Videos: Don't just rent 'em for entertainment! Analyze everything. If you want, take notes. Reverse, fast-forward, and put into your internal fashion file just how Ann Margaret, for instance, does it—not only what she wears but how she wears it. Study the walks, poses, and facial expressions of the stars as well. Rehearse!

Art books, galleries, and museums: Ancient, classical, modern, post-modern, post-post-modern. Sexy (as in Vargas). Fashiony (as in Erté). Renaissance? Why not? You're a ravishing Renaissance woman, yes? Low art, high art, kitsch art. Whatever starts-your-heart art. Ideal for ideas, inspiration, and showing you how the concepts of beauty have changed through time and have been interpreted by artists.

Stages of Glamma

Oh, you beautiful doll! Now you know how to make yourself into anything you want. Put it to the test and invent an incredible look for a very special evening. Take a full six hours to pull it together. Of course, not every occasion requires six hours of primping, fussing, pampering, dressing. Still, a true Style Siren never goes public without the appropriate preparations. There are different stages of glamma that don't demand much time at all:

Beach Glamma: High-heeled mules, sunglasses, sunscreen, lip line and fill in, waterproof mascara, and a suit with a chiffon sarong (work that sarong, gorge!). (Time elapsed: thirty minutes.)

Trip-to-the-deli Glamma: Essential, not just for the beefy stock boy but for that special someone who might also have to have Oreos with his morning coffee. So simple—powder, hat, or headwrap scarf, movie-star style, sunglasses, and lipstick. (Time elapsed: ten minutes.)

Coffee Klatch Glamma: A truly confident babe dresses for herself first, for men second, and for her buddy-babes last. But there's a certain kind of glam for those girls-only get-togethers that usually center around coffee (for, as we all know, where there's life, there's coffee), boys, business, and the business of boys. Some prefer to call the exchanges "teas." They can be performed at the babe-with-the-biggest-place place, or in one of the oldest, best hotels in town, or at a diner with excellent coffee. It's impossible to make these klatches happen during business hours or after an exhausting day at work. No, this is a special event for a non-working Saturday when at least six of you are available at once. Accept no cancellations! Pick a theme and dress appropriately:

1. Everyone-Wear-Her-Most-Recently-Purchased-Garment Theme.
2. Formal-Attire Theme (self-explanatory).
3. Dress-Against-Type Theme. (For instance, the hot, sexy, flirty femme becomes a chic butch Ms.)

These dress-up and discuss events do require prep time. The looks must allow for sitting and must not be destroyed if a little coffee slush or spill happens. (Time elapsed—one to three hours.)

Flash Hair Salon Glamma: Organizing your hair before getting your hair done is like organizing the house before the maid comes . . . you do it. Apply light foundation (best for shampoo drips), and keep lips, eyes, and cheeks subtle. Wear something that unzips or unbuttons easily so there's no do-damage. (Time elapsed—two hours without headscarf, forty-five minutes with.)

Politically Correct Glamma (Clothing for Your Causes): Stay-on-all-day but simple makeup—just a little, so your face changes expression when you do. Dress in clean, clear, direct, and comfortably polished fashion with freedom of movement. Of course, HHs—but with marching power. (Time elapsed: one hour, including the pressing of all garments.)

The Black Dress

An everybabe must-have. Women through the ages have been Style Sirens with this wardrobe staple. Take La Pasionaria, for instance, leader in the Spanish Civil War on the side of the socialists, she only wore black dresses. She lost the war, but kept the look—and reputation—through her forty years of self-imposed exile in Russia and her final years in Spain, after its liberation. At age ninety-four, she still wore those black dresses. This committed leader and black-dress-wearer is a style example to us all.

Another black-dress-wearer of worth was "The Lady in the Raven Dress." In the olden courts of Austrian aristocracy, balls and galas were glorious and happened often. They were spectaculars one would clamor to be invited to and spend twelve hours getting ready for (we would be scoffed at for only taking six!). One incredibly sweet, beautiful, and insecure legendary lovely came to a ball in a stunning black brocade satin gown trimmed with jewels and beads, with shoes and bag to match, natch. She was so luscious to look at, so much fun, that soon she was invited to everything. Her blood was blue—but she was flat busted (not SBB, broke!).

Wearing her only dress "the black dress" or "the raven dress," she attended every ball, having all of nobility on its knees with her glorious style and reputation. The dress, she believed, held the magical power of her social success.

Jealously ruled in those catty courts, and a particular sourpuss non-babe stole the dress and destroyed it. Though the Lady of the Raven Dress had acquired a fortune in gifts from admirers and could easily have had fifty dresses in any color made up, this poor, insecure, sweet babe naively believed that the dress was the source of her allure, and she saw the demise of her dress as a sign to retire from her social swirl.

With her wealth, like many retired goddesses (Lana Turner and her

Me in my little black dress.

llama ranch; Doris Day, the animal activist; Brigitte Bardot, who donated about half of her estate to an auction for animal protection funds), the lady of the Raven Dress raised horses—Lippizaners, you know, those huge, white Austrian ones with long white tails and manes—and from then on she never wore the same dress twice.

The Rubber Dress

The rubber dress existed in fetish-fashion for years, especially in London. I won't say that I made the rubber dress mainstream, but brought it out of the dark and into the night, when I took the look from London to New York. Then I became obsessed with wearing rubber and had the dresses custom-made. One of my dresses is in the collection of Billy Boy of Paris, who exhibits internationally famous people's famous style signatures from all time periods, bringing the rubber dress into fashion eternity. You can buy them off the racks in various places, and order them from Kim West, 9A Boundary Street, London E2, England U.K., who makes the tank dress in all colors including Bubblegum Pink. You'll feel as if you're wearing a hug . . . once you get it on, that is. Here's how:

Supplies: Turtle Wax Black Chrome Bumper Guard (for shining the outside). Baby powder or any other good-smelling powder (to slide on the inside).

Pre-game tips: Avoid garter belt and stockings unless you want your U-world hardware to show (which is good, too). Naked underneath is great in rubber, because it lifts and smooths every part of you, and it feels as good as it looks.

1 Powder the inside of the dress generously.
2 Starting from the bottom, step inside.

MARCUS LEATHERDALE

3 Now, roll the dress up. Watch your nails—if the rubber rips, you're finished.
4 Hook straps over shoulders. Arrange boobs.
5 Now, with gentle pinches, pull the rubber away from your body and adjust and smooth out air bubbles.
6 Apply Bumper Guard generously with a soft cloth all over. Watch out for streaks! Enlist assistance from GG for places you can't reach.

Everybody at the party will ask you how you got into that dress. Tell them to buy Brill's book if they want to know! Now, you will become moist underneath this dress, but it won't feel clammy; just slightly slippery. And when you remove the dress, your skin will feel smoother and softer than ever.

The Extra-Special, Mega-Important, You-Look-The-Most-Incredible-You've-Ever-Looked Glamma: The How to Get Dressed in Just Under Six Hours Technique

Let's say you're sort of seeing three GGs simultaneously. And as it happens, all three, of course, want to take you out for your birthday. What's a Brill babe to do? Well, you tell each one a different day is the B-day, natch! So every GG is happy and you're properly adored for your birthday week celebration. These events deserve your full six hours, as do any high-glam, fab functions worth your attendance. So, say he's picking you up at nine—the time to start primping, pampering, and getting dressed is three o'clock.

THINGS TO DO WHILE GETTING DRESSED

Perhaps you think spending six hours on getting dressed is an obscenely vain waste of time. It is obscenely vain. But not a waste of time. Besides, while you're hands are busy bedecking your fab face and body, you're mind is whirling away. Things to think about while your dressing:

1 Practice your spontaneous conversation. Talk for you and for him.

2 Drink coffee. Be sure to take breaks with your dressing and primping with ample doses of coffee and bottled water. Coffee gives you the serenity to dream it and the vitality to do it, as they say in those old coffee achiever commercials, and water purges the fabulous poison of coffee.
3 Take B-complex vitamins.
4 Think totally self-indulgent thoughts. Make a mental list of all the things you love about yourself.
5 Practice your poses and walks. There are different walks and poses for different outfits—skirt tightness and length, shoe shape and heel height, etc.—so make sure your walk and your pose appropriately accessorize your outfit.

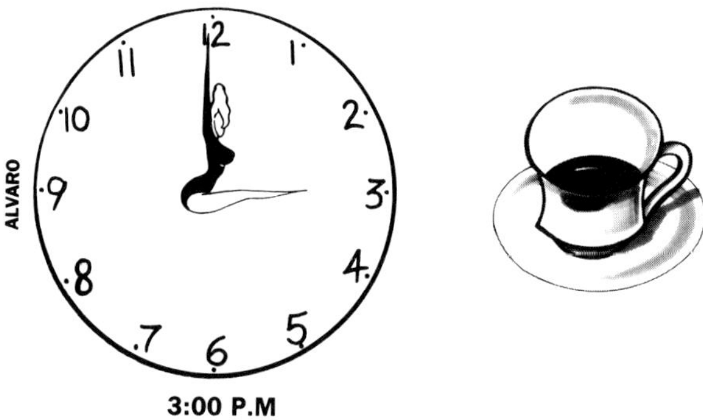

Thinking about getting dressed is the first step in getting dressed. Get into the dressing-up head. Surround yourself with the books, magazines, videos, and any other reference materials that relate to tonight's look. Peruse the books in a leisurely manner while listening to appropriate music—nothing too fast or loud (the idea is to build a music mood, going from gentle, pampering sounds to a grand entrance crescendo). Pop in a video (sound off) and study the moves while you polish your fingernails and toenails. Sip espresso carefully.

3:45 P.M.

Slip out of your maribou fantasy at-home loungewear and at-home-only HHs. Prepare for the Brill Babe's Bathing Ritual. Music: Increase the bass.

Brill Babe's Bathing Ritual

Peace. Quiet. Self-absorption. Self-indulgence. Lavish leisure. Your time. Totally. No phones (unless you want to pick up for a GG), no doorbells, no responsibilities, no obligations. You're free, because you're a "prisoner of the bubbles." That's what a bubble bath—and *every* bath is a bubble bath—means to a true babe. How to make your bubble bath an even more complete, sensual, spa-like experience:

1 Tubside Possibilities: Chilled extravagances (San Pellegrino water mixed with pear juice, Aqua Libre, Diet Coke, truffles). Scented candles. Potpourri (to add to the bubbly water). Cut lemons. Shaving supplies including Kiehl's Close Shavorettes Creme (write 109 Third Avenue, New York, NY 10003 for the Kiehl's catalogue—all their products are expensive but excellent) or Edge Shave Foam, and a sharp, fresh, double-blade razor such as Aftra.

2 Pre-Bath Pursuit-of-Angel-Skin Scrub: Prepare a mixture of a handful of kosher salt and regular salt. Add enough almond or olive oil to make a paste. Stand in the empty tub and splash a bit of water from the faucet onto your naked body. Then, take the paste and get scrubbing. All over. Everywhere. Boobs, bum, elbows . . . Shower off.

3 Don't-Hold-the-Mayo Hair Dip: Huge jar, cheap, fatty variety mayonnaise. Put all over dry hair. Ick! Take plastic wrap and make a turban around your head (for keeping body heat in and warming up the mayo conditioner). Then make another turban out of aluminum

foil with at least two pointed "ears" of folded foil (for fun!). Good substitute: Kiehl's Intensive Repairateur Deep Conditioning Pack (only don't shampoo, just rinse out after).

4 Le Masque de Mud: Appy French clay (available at any health food store) to clean face. Leave on till dry; rinse off with cool water.

5 Bubble Bath of Dreams: Adjust water temperature to your liking. Pour your favorite bubble bath and a package of that skin-softening miracle, Powdered Instant Milk, under running water. Fill that tub! Toss in some rose potpourri petals, just for effect. If your bubble bath does not impart a pink color, add a few drops of red food coloring, which will mingle with the milk into a creamy pink dream tub. Light candles. Climb in slowly. Inch down luxuriantly (up to the neck, watch those tinfoil "ears"!). Mmmnnn! Soak and relax. Add hot water as necessary. Bleach elbows with lemons. After fifteen minutes, shave legs and underarms. Massage feet. Stand up, drain tub. Shower off mud mask and hair dip. Shampoo and condition hair . . . *all* hair. Finish with a cool rinse. Tingly! Pat dry with fluffy towel. Smooth on body lotion (my favorites are Estée Lauder's Maximum Care Body Lotion and Revlon's Eterna 27 Enriched Body Moisturizer).

PAMPERING EXTRAS

1 Cream Cubes: Freeze sweet heavy cream in ice cube trays. Rub cubes over skin.

2 Vaseline Ruby Slippers: Glob Vaseline on feet. Slip feet into red cotton socks. Wear for hours while dressing.

3 Venus Mound Pomade: Rub a tiny amount of Vaseline into your palms and glaze it over your pubic hair, the ultimate in softening your purr-fur.

Perfume Layering

It's best to buy everything—soap, powder, perfume, and cologne spray—in your signature scent for tonight's GG (remember: same guy, same scent!). Perfume your pulsepoints—a little. Spray wet hair with cologne. Powder tender areas. (You've already soap-scented yourself in the bath.)

Makeup time! You've already planned your face in your head, so the look should come easy. Pump up the speed of your musical selection to get you through this high-activity primp-phase. Sit at your makeup table, wearing nothing but your smile and Vaseline Ruby Slippers (see box on Pampering Extras). I won't tell you how to do your look—you know what's hot for tonight—but I have some suggestions:

The Neo-Cleo Glamma-Eyes

Supplies: Eyelash glue. Waterproof mascara. Eyelash curler. Medium and long individual false eyelashes. Slant-angle eyeshadow brush. Dark gray or black eyeshadow. Face powder. Powder brush. Q-tips. Espresso. ***Technique:*** You know when you were a kiddle and made all those great faces in the mirror? You'd skwoosh your features in all directions in search of yet another funny face. What about the one where you'd take one finger at the outer corner of the eye and slant it out and up all the way? That's the position to create Neo-Cleo Glamma Eyes.

1 Get out the angle shadow brush. Dab the brush lightly in the dark eyeshadow. Place the point of the brush against the center of your

upper eyelid and paint out. Repeat. Touch up the top outer corners with more shadow to fill in where you missed. You're after an angled-up, slanted cat-eye line. Sexy, sexy! Sip espresso. Do other eye.

2 Dip your powder brush in a little loose face powder. Softly dust powder over entire eye. Sip espresso. Other eye.

3 Add a little powder under the base of the lower lashes with a Q-tip. Sip espresso. Other eye.

4 Now shadow-line the lower lid with dark shadow. Begin at the center and move in a straight line to the outer corner. Be sure that there's a space between the upper lid and lower lid lines—don't let the lines meet. Sip espresso. Other eye.

5 Apply mascara to bottom lashes.

6 Curl top lashes.

7 Apply mascara to upper lashes.

8 Add three individual lashes, dipped in eyelash glue, to the outer corners of each eye a little further out at the end of your natural eyelash line to widen and upsweep your eyes. There: flawlessly feline fabulous. Purr in the mirror. Take a minute and just adore. (Remove later with oil based make-up remover.)

The Eyebrow for the Highbrow Babe

How is it those swingin' sisters get their eyebrows to do that "thang"? You know, go up and arch over like that! Well, some get the look by shaving off half the brow and drawing in the rest (oh, no!) or by the 1950s stencil-brow technique. But these methods are dated and dangerous. Shave the brows and they might not grow back—and stenciling may be your only option. There are wonderful ways to give you the shape and shade of brows your lovely eyes deserve.

My best friend Janis is obsessed with the "What if" scenario, as in "What if you were stranded on an island and could only bring two beauty items with you, what would they be?" Hers would be a tweezer and the Maybelline eyebrow kit. Why? Her sexy way of arching her arched brow is her never-miss seduction trick. (I said what if she was stuck on an island, but I didn't say she had to be stuck there *alone.*)

My favorite brows are raised high arches. Here's the equipment list:

1 Stiff, angled eyebrow brush.
2 Matte shadow powder in blonde, auburn, black, brown, or charcoal. (Note: Maybelline's Brush-On Brow Kit contains angled brush and shadow and it's small, cheap, and excellent.)
3 Toothbrush (cleaned with hot water and soap after every use).
4 Tweezer.
5 Astringent.
6 Stiff hair spray or hair gel.
7 Baby powder.
8 Mirror (natch!).

Creating the High Arches

1 Pluck stray hairs from under the brows and between them if necessary. Please, tweeze carefully and never overpluck. When you get to the place just parallel to the outside corner of your eye, pluck with a slightly heavier hand to taper the brow up and out (think Spock of "Star Trek"). Use astringent over plucked area; then baby powder the area. Make a decaf espresso (you need a steady hand!), then return to the mirror.
2 Dip the angle brow brush into the correct color brow shadow. Starting from the inner corner of the brow, brush up, concentrating on the upper portion of the brow. Stop at the highest point of the arch (parallel to the outside corner of the eye). At that point, exaggerate the arch by making a peak on top with shadow—it should be angular, not rounded. Now feather the shadow line down a bit and out.

3 Spritz the toothbrush with hairspray (or apply a bit of gel to the bristles). Brushing up, go over the entire brow to groom well, and gently set into position.
4 Usage: When you see a GG walk past you, lift those raised high arches his way. Does he double back or pause a second to look again in your direction? Yeah? Then you've got it!

The Brill-Burn Mouth

Here's how to kiss-proof your lipstick no matter how many lip-print tattoos (or in my case, Brill Burns) you're giving.

Supplies:

- Waterproof lip liners (Revlon makes a great one), one slightly lighter than your lipstick shade, and another three tones darker.

- Lipstick in a drop-dead glamma color and of a somewhat dry, not moist, formula (you can leave moist lipsticks uncovered overnight to dry them out).

- Clear lip gloss (optional).

Technique:

1 You've already applied foundation and lightly brushed on powder to the entire face, lips included. With the slightly lighter lip pencil, line your upper and lower lips.
2 Completely fill in lips with lighter lip pencil.
3 Take darker pencil and darken the center part of your lower lip, going inside the mouth a bit. Notice: Instant pout!
4 Pat on a little face powder.
5 Dot lipstick onto lips. Blend with finger.
6 Apply a thin coat of lip gloss if you like.

6:45 P.M.

Now do your hair. Slow-burn music is best for this tactile activity, something bluesy-chantoosy, like Peggy Lee. Be sure you have access to mirrors at all angles.

High Hair: How to do the Brilldo

There are lots of reasons to try a new do. Say you're in one of those "Teflon times"—you know, when no one or nothing seems to stick. It's time to change—and only more will do. So how about high hair? I like mine really high, but depending on the length of your hair and the state of your mind, you may go a tier or two lower.

Equipment:

- Skinny bobby pins that match your haircolor (if blonde, get silver). How many? Too many.
- Stiff-holding hair spray.
- Smoothing hair brush with fine bristles.
- Coated rubber band.

- Height device: Either a pair of pantyhose (finally, a constructive use for 'em) that is close to your hair color, or write to: T.O.D. c/o B.R.A.T.S., Accessory Division, 421 Hudson St., Suite 601, N.Y., N.Y. 10014. Ask for the catalogue with the "French Hair Flair" nylon mesh poufs and doughnutpoufs. (You can buy a few and stack and pin them together for really high hair.)

Directions:

1 Bow your head and brush hair forward to cover your face.
2 Place the height device on the crown of your head. Insert bobby pins all the way around the border of height device (if using hose, poke holes through fabric) to fasten firmly to your head.
3 Lift your head while lifting all your hair up with both hands to cover height device.
4 Place rubber band over hair right in the center on top of height device. Be sure eveything feels taut and firmly in place.
5 Slip out a small section of hair carefully. Wrap it around the rubber band to hide the evidence. Pin in place.
6 Arrange strands that are sticking up out of rubber band in little curls or into a small French roll; tuck into the back and pin. Optional: pull down a few bangs in front or tendrils around your face and neck.
7 Use brush to gently glaze the surface of the do, to smooth away separation between strands.
8 Spray away!

Sex and Wigs

We know that natural hair only gets sexier with sex. Oh, that just-laid look! But what about falls, braids, ponytails, and hairpieces—you know, wigs, that fabulous faux hair, look-altering staple? A GG will love you in different lengths and colors of hair. Wear wigs for him, in your "natural color," or any shade you please, just for one night. It's swingin'! Wigs are not only for religious sects and bald people—they're fashion freedom.

Just-for-fun fun. Great-for-sex fun. Of course, wigs should be sex-proofed, as this little anecdote reveals:

I was in Miami, staying at a villa with a sauna and hot tub in the bathroom. I was about to slip into the tub, in preparation for my boyfriend's arrival. Since I knew my GG wouldn't wait downstairs but would come up to "surprise" me in the tub, I made sure to be made up and wigged first. The hairpiece I chose was an ultra-long Mermaid number, a real waterfall of hair, to suit the surroundings. As I suspected, my GG entered the bathroom while I was enjoying my soak. He scooped me out of the tub and onto the tiles. The door was closed. The tub was rising. And our love, of course, was volcanic, too.

Dreamy? Yes. But, as you know, synthetic fake hair is made from plastic. Fine threads of plastic. And plastic melts under extreme heat. Next thing I knew, I was dreadlocked from sex. My silky synthetic strands had melted into a Rasta symphony! Now I know to wear human hair (such as the "caviar of hair," which comes from the virgin—and I do mean virgin—hair of Tuscany nuns before they take their vows) in such steamy situations. But, despite my meltdown, the hairpiece never came off my head, because I had sex-proofed it. To do this:

1 Section by section, tease your own hair in the area where you'll attach the hairpiece.

2 Connect the faux hair to the roots of your hair by X-pinning in place one bobbypin under and one bobbypin over. You can't overpin. So for extra safety "x"-tra pin.

7:45 P.M.

Refresh your fragrance (perfume your pulsepoints, cologne-ize your hair, spritz your chiffon pocket square). Now you're ready for the action music—very active club music—whatever you love to dance to at the moment.

Now, doll, dress! In this order:

1 Enter your U-world. Garter belt, stockings, HHs, G-string, bra. Clock the action in the mirror. Set the self-timer on the Polaroid and snap yourself in various poses—the ultimate in narcissistic indulgence. Love yourself!

2 Slip on the glorious garment. Walk around in it. Break it in. Rule in it! Get used to wearing it, so that the dress doesn't wear you—you wear the dress!

3 Accessorize. Sparingly. Choose accessories that you really like, not what happens to be the fashion of the minute. Your inner and outer glamma are astonishing, and only a few bits of scarf, headband, jewel, handbag, etc. are called for. After you accessorize, remove the last thing you put on. You don't need it.

8:50 P.M.

Change all the light bulbs to soft red. Hide all your beauty evidence inside the bathtub and draw the curtain. Gather the trail of coffee cups throughout the house and stash them in kitchen cabinet. In other words—redecorate! Spritz cologne through the air—even in the outer hallway. Change music back to smoldery sounds. Turn down volume on phone and answering machine. Take a deep breath and hold it, so that when the doorbell rings you'll be flushed and breathless. You'll feel a sweet warm happiness that's your inner and outer glamma in full bloom. Strike a pose. Let down your guard. Share the wealth of your gorgeousness.

May the celebration begin! You can relax, because you are now a real Ms. Natural Resources, like I promised. And in just under six hours!

WALTER RAMBALDINI

Ms. Natural Resources

. . . and in

"just under six hours."